D1830317

PRE-MUSSALMAN INDIA

PRE-MUSSALMAN INDIA

A HISTORY OF THE MOTHERLAND PRIOR TO THE SULTANATE OF DELHI

M. S. NATESON

GYAN

Published by

Gyan Publishing House
5, Ansari Road
Daryaganj, New Delhi-110002
Phone: 011-47034999, 9811692060
E-mail: books@gyanbooks.com

Distribution Network
gyanbooks.com
India, USA, Canada, UK, Australia, France

© Publisher
All rights reserved. No part of this work may be reproduced, stored, adapted, or transmitted in any form or by any means, electronic, mechanical, photocopying, micro-filming, recording or otherwise, or translated in any language, without the prior written permission of the copyright owner and the publisher.

ISBN : 978-81-212-3917-2 (PB)
First Published, Srirangam, 1917

2nd Impression 2020

Printed at: Gyan Press, Delhi.

The book is sold subject to the condition that it shall not, by way of trade or otherwise, be lent, resold, hired out, or otherwise circulated without the prior publisher's written consent.

Pre-Mussalman India
Author: M. S. Nateson

PRE-MUSSALMAN INDIA

A History of the Motherland Prior to the Sultanate of Delhi

BY

M. S. NATESON,

Teacher, Hindu Secondary School,

Trichinopoly.

SRIRANGAM:

SRI VANI VILAS PRESS.

1917.

AVANT PROPOS.

Dear and impartial reader,

Despite the brave homilies on virtue which abound, this is a world in which a man may be too good and too intelligent and become an object of distrust to those who never lay themselves open to this accusation. The most misgiving reader need not be afraid of the present writer. He is not too good, nor is he too intelligent.

An author, however he may disown it, will certainly be suspected of some egotism when he begins to tell his thoughts to the world and record them in a permanent form. He can hardly presume that the world has an interest in his thoughts, without taking it for granted that they have some importance. A favourite way of parrying this inference is to represent that what the author has done has been urged on him by others. Yet a book is never published "by request". It may therefore be safely said that the author has requested himself to do it.

This book proposes to introduce the reader to the distant past of India, prior to 1206 A. D., the era of the first Sultanate of Delhi. India is a sacred land, whosoever stands on which, whether alien or a child of the soil, feels himself surrounded—unless his soul is degraded to the level of brute animals—by the living thoughts of the earth's best and purest sons who have been working to raise the animal to the Divine through centuries whose beginning history fails to trace. India's very air is full of the pulsations of spirituality. India is sacred to philosophy, to ethics and spirituality, to all that tends to give a respite to man in his incessant struggle for the preservation of the animal, to all training that makes man throw off the garment of animalism and stand revealed as the spirit immortal, the birthless, the deathless, the ever-blessed.

"This is the land where the cup of pleasure was full and fuller has been the cup of misery, until here, first of all, man found out that it was all vanity ; here, first of all, in the prime of youth, in the lap of luxury, in the height of glory and plenitude of power, man broke through the fetters of delusion. Here, in this ocean of humanity, amidst the sharp interaction of strong currents of pleasure and pain, of strength and weakness, of joy and sorrow, of smile and tear, of life and death, in the melting rhythm of eternal peace and calmness, arose the throne of RENUNCIATION! Here, in this land, the great problems of life and death, of the thirst for life and the vain mad struggles to preserve it, resulting in the accumulation of woes, were first grappled with and solved—solved as they never were before and never will be hereafter ; for, here and here alone was discovered that even life itself is an evil, the shadow only of something which is real. This is the land where alone Religion was practical and real, and here alone men and women plunged boldly in to realise the goal, just as in other lands they madly plunge in to realise the pleasures of life. Here and here alone the human heart has expanded, till it included not only humanity, but birds, beasts and plants; from the highest gods to grains of sand, the highest and the lowest all find a place in the heart of man, grown great, infinite. And here alone the human soul studied the universe as one unbroken unity whose every pulse was its own pulse.

"As far back as the days of the Upanishads, we have thrown the challenge to the world न धनेन न प्रजया त्यागेनैकेन अमृतत्वमानशुः—Not by wealth, not by progeny, but by Renunciation alone is immortality reached. Race after race has taken the challenge up, and tried its utmost to solve the world-riddle on the plane of desires. The attempts have all failed. The question has yet to be decided whether peace will survive or war, patience or non-forbearance, goodness or wickedness, muscle or brain, worldliness or spirituality. We have solved our problem ages ago, and hold on to it through good or evil fortunes and mean to hold on to it till the end of time. Our solution is Unworldliness—Renunciation."

One point to which the reader's attention should be invited is the extreme originality of the publication. The author dares to ask if the Aryans ever came into India as a conquering race. He knows that the institution of Varnasrama prevalent among the Aryans from prehistoric times gives a direct lie to any theory, however well-propounded, that the Aryans are foreigners to India. He also thinks that the European nations, as also the Turks and the Persians, however sincerely particular men may cherish particular pet theories of their own, are not Aryans. The greatest authorities for the Aryan in this respect are his sacred books where not an iota of evidence is found to prove that the Aryan ever came into India from a foreign country. And the life-story of Gautama the Buddha, and his gospel of love and toleration—how grossly misrepresented by interested aliens—it hardly passes one's understanding to conceive !

Herbert Spencer says that that which constitutes history, properly so called, is the natural history of society. The only history that is of practical value is what may be called descriptive sociology. And the highest office which the historian can discharge is that of so narrating the lives of nations as to furnish materials for a comparative sociology, and for the subsequent determination of the ultimate laws to which social phenomena conform. The author leaves it to the reader to judge how far he has stuck to the definition given above.

Facts are merely the tools in the hands of the intelligent historian. He has to and he should teach the supreme value of accuracy and permanently impress the same on children's minds. Children should not be made to sit in judgment over great historical characters and sum up their verdict in a well-chosen word or a few well-chosen words of approval or condemnation. To the great dead they must offer their admiration, their gratitude where they can,—and if not, their silence. *De mortuis nil nisi bonum.* They may not presume to judge their forefathers, but they may and must judge the issues that confronted them.

The true historian is a prophet, a man in whom the past calls to the present and the present calls to the future. History gives a season ticket over the railways of the past. The main principle of teaching history should be to concentrate the mind on the forces and influences that have made and are making the nation.

" History is a pageant as well, and the teacher must never lose sight of the fact that behind the pageant is the process, that all the noise and colour and movement mean something. The pageantry of history is sacramental, it has an inward spiritual import that redeems it from a charge of nothingness. It is a great religious drama that moves on from age to age with the world for its stage and all humanity for its actors, and who knows what assemblage of unseen spectators is beyond the footlights? Unless a teacher feels something at least of this spiritual significance of history, he had better not teach history at all. The vocation of a history teacher is one of the highest to which a man or a woman might be called,—the revelation of God."

The author believes that he has sufficiently explained to the reader the thoughts that underlie the publication of this book. If the following few pages will arouse in the reader's mind a few thoughts which would eventually direct him to understand history aright, which would make him realise for himself the purpose of all history and which would enthuse him to do actions worthy of the descendents of the heroes of antiquity who form the theme of this book, the author's ambition will be more than fulfilled.

The author would only like to add that a book of a similar character would have been of no mean service to him when he was young, as this peradventure may be to many now.

The author begs to remain,
Gentle and dear reader,
Ever yours in the Lord of the Universe,

TRICHINOPOLY,
April 1917.

M. S. Nateson

To

His Holiness

The Illustrious Sri Swami Vivekananda

of green and glorious memory,

the inspirer of modern India,

to the cause He represented,

to all His Disciples, Followers and Admirers,

and to the work in which they are all

engaged heart and soul,

this little book

is dedicated

in all humility and reverence

for the propagation of the Truth.

ॐ

भारतीयमताचार-
स्थापनोदितमूर्तये ।
विवेकानन्दयतये
तच्छात्राणां च भूतये ।
चरित्रमेतद्राचितं
भारतीयं पुरातनम् ।
अर्पितं विदुषां प्रीत्यै
भूयादाचन्द्रतारकम् ॥

CONTENTS.

INTRODUCTION.

A correct and reliable history of India has yet to be written. Not only individual peculiarities of temperament, but also in-born prejudices and other defects have, in the absence of trustworthy records, all combined to minimise the historical value of most books on the subject. This is especially true of the earliest or the Hindu period. Many fanciful theories started over a hundred years ago have, with slight alterations to suit later so-called ethnological conclusions, been accepted and repeated by later writers; and they are now put down in ordinary text-books as if they are all proved history. The fact, however, is that no European has yet correctly understood Indian Vedic literature, nor the true origin and principles of the caste system which has played such a great part in the building of Indian civilisation. That is because the European

Orientalist, however patient his search, however deep his linguistic lore, has never approached Indian sacred literature with the unprejudiced mind, humility and reverence necessary for the seeker after truth ; he has had too lofty a sense of his own superior civilisation, too much confidence in his own wisdom and capacity for critical judgment ; this vanity has quite warped his vision. The result has been that many theories which at best are only ingenious guesses have, by being constantly repeated by so-called authorities, come to be regarded as more or less established facts ; and are put in as such, without any qualifications, in ordinary text-books. A few instances should suffice taken at random from a text-book otherwise well-written. "The immigration of the Aryans into India must have commenced about 1500 years before Christ." "The religion of the Aryans consisted in the worship of what was awe-inspiring or what struck them as specially beautiful or beneficial in nature. They prayed to the sun and the clouds, fire and thunder, the dawn and the bright sky." As the Aryans spread eastwards they became less cheerful and vigourous, more ritualistic and priest-ridden "and were infected with gloomy aboriginal beliefs." "The caste distinction was at first mainly ethnological. The fair-skinned Aryan felt the utmost repugnance for the dark and stunted savage (non-Aryan)." Buddhism was "essentially a religion of the people as opposed to Brahmanism the religion of a caste." "To people so smothered in superstition and so credulous as the bulk of the natives of India, an Impersonal faith such as Buddhism could not carry strong conviction," and so Buddhism declined. All such generalisations may be ingenious enough ; but, why in the name of innocence should Indian boys be taught to believe in all such obiter dicta ? Will it not be more praiseworthy for a compiler to state at once that there are no materials to construct the earliest periods of Indian history, and to begin the account from 600 B. C. as Mr. Vincent Smith has rightly done ? Indeed it has always struck me that the opening chapters in almost every text-book on Indian history placed in the hands of school children—all the chapters dealing with the history of India prior to Alexander's invasion—should be completely deleted, as not being based on proved facts. I have no objection to grown-up men discussing the theories of Orientalists; but such theories do great harm intellectually when put down to be learnt as facts by unsuspecting school children.

I am very glad therefore that Mr. M. S. Nateson has written the history of "Pre-Mussalman India" keeping in the background all the harmful theories I have referred to. I have gone through the greater part of Mr. M. S. Nateson's compilation, and find that he has taken great pains to emphasise the more salient and permanent features of Indian civilisation. He has in the main diligently eschewed all objectionable and doubtful matter. A school-book of this kind is a great desideratum;

I trust therefore that this will receive the patronage it so well deserves. I have suggested to the author that for the benefit of the lower forms he should speedily bring out vernacular editions of his book I have no doubt he will do so if he gets sufficient encouragement.

OTTAPPALAM,
April 1917.

M. Krishnamacharya, B.A.,L.T.,
Headmaster, The High School,
Ottappalam.

ॐ

॥ श्रीगुरुभ्यो नमः ॥

CHAPTER I.

The Age of the Itihasas.

1. There is no history of India, strictly speaking, prior to the Mahamadan conquest. The non-Aryan peoples of India, the present-day animists, were too little civilised to be able to record their history. And the history of the Aryans has to be pieced together into a connected story from their sacred literature, portions of which relate to a time previous to 2000 B. C.

2. **Aryans and non-Aryans:**—There are various theories about the ancient homes of the Aryans. The steppes of central Asia, the Arctic regions, and the borders of the Swiss lakes have often been spoken of as the original homes of the Aryans, both eastern and western. There are other theories that the Indo-

Aryans were a conquering race who took possession of the lands of the non-Aryan peoples whom they killed or exterminated. But the Varnasrama Dharma, prevalent among the Aryans from prehistoric times lown to the present day, recognised even by western orientalists, makes us question the relevancy of this latter theory. The civilisation of the ancient Aryans, their system of Government, their peaceful pursuits, their agricultural operations, their industrial arts, their righteous wars, and above all, their religion, as proved by the sacred books of the Hindus and by the political division of Aryavarta into the 56 kingdoms of yore, go clearly to prove that, from prehistoric times, the Aryans have been living on the banks of the Sindhu and the Ganga. And Afghanistan was a portion of ancient India. The animist non-Aryan tribes, traces of whom still exist, were gradually absorbed into the Aryan fold. The worship of some of the animist deities by the Hindus of today also shows that the ancient Aryans converted the animists very slowly and gradually, keeping up portions of their rituals so as not to make them feel alien in the Aryan camp even as the Roman Catholic Christians do today in the case of converts.

3. **The caste system:**—It is not possible to make any definite statement on this point. The Hindus believe that the human soul takes birth in a particular caste as the result of actions based upon certain qualities in a previous incarnation. When the system originated cannot be precisely stated. The declaration of Sri Krishna in the Bhagavad Gita is "The fourfold caste was created by me by the differentiation of *guna* and *karma*." The diversity of human temperaments and tendencies is the cause of this division. All men are not of the same nature because of the preponderance of the different gunas in them. Manu says that the four castes are Veda-ordained.

4. The caste system was meant to make perfect the growth of humanity, by the

special culture of certain features, through the process of discriminate selection. It was probably the result of long ages of karmic evolution by which certain natures were specially fitted to do certain actions.

5. Nor can it be stated with any precision whether intercourse among the various castes was at all permitted in ancient India. While varnasankara was held in great dread, a certain latitude did certainly exist for one class to take upon itself the duties of another, if a particular individual who desired the change was capable physically and intellectually to discharge the duties of a higher class.

6. The duties of the four castes are thus stated by Manu :

Brahman:—Teaching, Study, Sacrifice, conducting sacrifice, charity, and receiving gifts.

Kshatriya:—Protection of people, charity, sacrifice, study, and non-attachment to sense-objects.

Vaisya:—Protection of domestic animals, charity, sacrifice, study, trade, banking, and agriculture.

Sudra:—Service, free from malice, to the other castes.

But greater than the Brahman was the scholar, विद्वत्सु कृतबुद्धयः, कृतबुद्धिषु कर्तारः, and कर्तृषु ब्रह्मवेदिनः ।

7. The Brahman was the supreme teacher and the custodian of Dharma. He alone was competent to preserve it. He should not take upon himself other duties ; nor should he seek honour and fame on any account ; these were to be shunned as poison.

8. It is not open to the student of history to say whether the Varnasrama Achara was based upon the principle of division of labour or not. although the scheme tended in time to become hereditary, based solely on birth, and certain professions were monopolised by certain classes of the community.

9. Itihasas or History:— The Ramayana:—The Ramayana is a most unique work. The Samhitas, the Aranyakas, the Smrities, the Mahabbharata, and even the Puranas are not regarded by the Hindus in the same light as the Ramayana. These former are accessible only to a very few, an infinitesimal minority of the Brahmans. But the Ramayana is a work that gives a man everything he holds dear and valuable in this world and leads him to the feet of the Almighty. There is almost no Hindu home where the Ramayana, in some form or other, complete or incomplete, is not found. When any one desires to know the result of a contemplated project, he desires a child to open a page of the Ramayana and decides by the nature of the subject dealt with therein. The work has been translated into almost all the languages of India and also into Italian, French, Latin and English.

There also exist other Ramayanas than *the Ramayana*. The Ananda Ramayana, the Adhyatma Ramayana, and a host of others, in many languages besides Sanskrit, too numerous to mention, all depict the story of Valmiki; but Valmiki's is *the Ramayana* par excellence.

"The cloud-capped mountains, the swift-coursing rivers, nay, all created things shall pass away and be as nought. But the Ramayana shall outlive them and never fade from the hearts of men." This is the boon of immortality that the poem enjoys.

The heroes are the most perfect any one can conceive. The poem was composed when Sri Rama was yet upon the earth, when his deeds and fame were fresh in the hearts of men. It was sung before himself by his very sons. The poem was the first of its kind and an unapproachable ideal for all time to come, the best model for all future poets.

The main theme of the poem is the story of prince Sri Rama who was driven into exile with his wife and brother. In the course of his wanderings Sri Rama suffered the loss of his consort who was carried off by the Rakshasa king Ravana of Ceylon. But Sri Rama crossed the narrow straits and, after many adventures in which his enemy Ravana was killed, rescued his wife. The period of exile being over, Sri Rama returned to his capital and was crowned king. The people began to murmur that Sita must be divorced because she had lived in the house of Ravana. In order to satisfy the demands of an ignorant populace, Sita, who was expecting soon to become a mother, was banished into a forest where she was received by the sage Valmiki as a guest. She was delivered of two boys, Kusa and Lava, to whom the sage taught the poem. The boys recited the thrilling incidents of Sri Rama's life in his presence, and Sri Rama longed to take Sita back Sita appeared and appealed to the gods to testify to her innocence. The earth opened, Vasundhara appeared, took Sita on her lap and vanished into the bosom of the earth. And Sri Rama, over-whelmed with grief, received celestial intimation that his mission on earth was finished and he was to return to heaven. He plunged into the Sarayu and rose no more.

This is the ancient epic of India. Sri Rama was the embodiment of truth, of morality. He was the ideal son, the ideal husband, the ideal father, and above all, the ideal king. "No language can be purer, none chaster, none more beautiful, and at the same time simpler, than the language in which the great poet has depicted the life of Sri Rama. And what to speak of Sita? The literature of the world that is past may be exhausted, but it is certain that the literature of the world of the future will have also to be exhausted before another Sita could be found. Sita is unique; that character was depicted once and for all. There may have been several Ramas, perhaps, but never more than one Sita! She is the very type of the true Indian woman, for, all the Indian ideals of a perfected woman have grown out of that one life of Sita; and here she stands these thousands of years, commanding the worship of every man, woman and child, throughout the length and breadth of the land of Aryavarta. There she will always be, this glorious Sita, purer than purity itself, all patience and all suffering. She who suffered that life of suffering without a murmur, she is the ever-chaste and ever-pure wife, she the ideal of the people, the ideal of the gods, the great Sita, India's national god she must always remain. And every Hindu knows her too well to require much delineation. All Hindu mythology may vanish, even the Vedas may depart, and the Sanskrit language may vanish for ever, but so long as there will be five Hindus speaking the most vulgar patois, there will be the story of Sita present. Sita has gone into the very vitals of the Hindu race. She is there in the blood of every Hindu man and woman; all Hindus are the children of Sita. Any attempt to modernise Hindu women, if it tries to take them apart from that ideal of Sita, is immediately a failure, as is seen every day. The women of

India must grow and develop in the foot-prints of Sita, and that is the only way."

10. The Mahabharata:—The Mahabharata is a much bigger epic and is of a much later origin than the Ramayana. It contains the story of a race descended from King Bharata who was the son of Dushyanta and Sakuntala. The ponderosity of the epic has long been an obstacle to its main and subsidiary morals enjoying a wide circulation except among the purely Sanskrit scholars. The work consists of 18 parvas and describes in detail the war between two families of cousins, the Kauravas and the Pandavas, for the throne of Indraprastha, the modern Delhi. There are many other incidents mentioned in the work, besides, and it would take too long even to briefly hint at them. The student of history should therefore restrict himself to the main theme of the poem. Duryodhana was mortally jealous of his cousin Yudhishthira and his brothers and wished to do away with them by any means fair or foul. His indulgent father, the blind old man, could not overrule his wayward son. All his attempts foiled, Duryodhana challenged his cousin to play dice with Sakuni, Duryodhana's uncle and evil genius. Yudhishthira could not in honour refuse the challenge; he played and lost. His kingdom, his brothers, himself and even his wife were staked and all were lost. One more throw of dice witnessed the Pandava's defeat; Yudhishthira and his brothers and wife had to retire to the forests for 12 years and then live in a city incognito for a year before the kingdom could be restored. His part of the pledge having been faithfully fulfilled, Yudhishthira sent Sri Krishna as ambassador to Duryodhana to re-claim his kingdom, but the headstrong Duryodhana would not yield without fight even as much land as a needle's point would hold. So, at last, preparations were made on both sides for war and all the rulers of India took part in it, one side or the other. The combatants-in-arms met each other at Kurukshetra and fought for 18 days.

393,660 chariots, as many elephants, 1,180,980 horse and 1,968,300 foot were assembled on that awful field of carnage. Hero after hero fell till Duryodhana's death decided the issue in favour of the Pandavas. Of the many millions that were assembled only very few men were left alive. Yudhishthira performed the Aswamedha and ascended the throne of his ancestors. 36 years later, Sri Krishna left his mortal body and the Pandavas, having seated Parikshit on the throne, retired to the Himalayas on the great journey, the Mahaprasthana. Yudhishthira in his mortal body proceeded to Heaven, his wife and brothers having given up their bodies on the way. He met his brothers, now immortals, and all at last is bliss.

The great incident of the war was the marvellous and immortal poem of the Bhagavad Gita, the Song Celestial. It is the popular scripture of India and the loftiest of all teachings. It consists of a dialogue held by Arjuna with Sri Krishna, just before the commencement of the fight on the battlefield. Arjuna's lion-heart faltered and he sank despondent on the floor of his chariot, Not from fear, or the sight of his foes in serried array, not from terror of death, nor of warrior's charge, failed that heroic heart. But for the impending slaughter of relatives, of comrades, of boyhood's dear companions and the friends of maturer years, of fathers, grandfathers, uncles and teachers, कृपया परयाविष्टः, the iron heart of the warrior broke with anguish, "I will not fight" and he cast away his bow. Then the Lord, to cheer him, spake the wonderful song, the Song Celestial, that, uttered thousands of years ago, has since echoed from heart to heart, sweetest and loftiest of all teaching given to those who love the Lord.

Thus ends the story of "Virtue's Triumph". It is impossible to recount here even in the briefest outline the unending array of the grand and majestic characters of the mighty heroes depicted by the genius and mastermind of

Vyasa. The majesty of Bhishma, the nobility of Yudhishthira, the peerlessness of Sri Krishna, and not less brilliant, the characters of the women, Gandhari, Kunti, Draupadi,—these and a hundred other characters have been the cherished heritage of the whole Hindu world for several thousands of years and form the basis of its thoughts and of its moral and ethical ideas. In fact, the Ramayana and the Mahabharata are the two encvolopaedias of ancient Aryan life and wisdom, portraying an ideal civilisation, which humanity has yet to aspire after.

11. Society in the epic age:—Both the epics reveal to us pictures of Hindu society as it existed in times gone by. All the ordinary features of present-day Hindu life are fully depicted and there are very little differences in manners and customs between ancient and the present-day Hindu society. The characteristic Hindu doctrines of karma and avatara are recognised in the poems as freely as they are today.

The feeling of the sacredness of the cow was then as strong as it is now.

12. Intellectual activity in the epic age:—These epics also reveal the fact that the intellectual activity of the Aryans was very great even as it is now. The Brahmans taught that learning was the highest and noblest possession of man and established throughout the country schools of philosophy, theology and law. The difficulties of language and the interpretation of obscure and difficult passages in the hymns made the Brahmans ingenious and subtle to a very great degree. The study of the stars also attracted their attention; in fact, considerable progress was made in it. Logic and mathematics were also subjects of study and research among them. Their chief delight, however, from the earliest times, was in philosophy. Metaphysical speculation was to them an absorbing passion. From a too engrossing attention to it they acquired an abstracted and impractical habit of mind to which in great measure is due their neglect of political science, perceptible even in the present day. But the mass of the people remained steeped in ignorance and a prey to superstition, till at length they came to look to the Brahmans for knowledge on all subjects and accepted without question what they chose to tell them. This popular ignorance made Sanskrit, a language of surpassing force and beauty, into a secret language of the priests, and although it served them as an almost perfect medium for the expression of their thoughts, served to create an air of mystery around them and to confine the knowledge of the Scriptures and of Brahman learning within the circle of their order. The gradual result of all this was that Sanskrit soon ceased to be a living language.

CAHPTER II.

The Dravidians.

13. The Aryan expansion in the south brought them in contact with people not less civilised than themselves, living in towns with settled forms of government. In the conflict of civilisations which followed, the superior Aryan came out successful, but the Dravidian did not succumb without leaving traces of its existence behind.

14. The Mixed race:—In the mixed race that arose from the union of the Aryan with the Dravidian, the preponderating element was Aryan civilisation and Aryan religion. In fact, the Aryan always took within his fold the genius born of other tribes, even outside the pale of his Varnasrama. As examples may be quoted Vasishtha, Narada, Visvamitra, Satyakama Jabala, Vyasa, Kripa, Drona, Karna and others of questionable parentage, who were raised to the position of the Brahman or the Kshatriya in virtue of their superior learning or valour.

15. Dravidian history :—Just as very little is known of the early history of the pure Aryan kingdoms of the north, so also very little is known of the early history of the Dravidio-Aryan kingdoms of the Cholas, the Pandyas and the Cheras of the south.

16. Dravidian civilisation :—That the Dravidian civilisation was in no way inferior to the Aryan may be proved from the extensive literature, chiefly Tamil, which includes epics, lyrics and philosophical poems. The later works show the influence of the Aryan civilisation on the Dravidian, because of the large number of Dravidianised Sanskrit words occurring in them.

CHAPTER III.

The Post-Vedic Ages.

17. More than 20 centuries had rolled by since the destruction of the ancient Kshatriya dynasties on the battlefield of Kurukshetra, and Hindu society had undergone a profound transformation in every feature,—home life, religious ideas, language, court life, etc. It will be the purpose of this chapter to determine the factors that operated to create this new India out of the materials supplied by the wreck of Kurukshetra.

18. After the final compilation of the Vedas by Vyasa, when the ancient type of political sovereignty was gradually disappearing, owing to the flooding of India's social life by new racial elements starting up into prominence from within and pouring forth across the frontiers, the old centres of Vedic orthodoxy were being swamped from all sides and had gradually to lead a sort of migratory and scattered existence, seeking the ægis of such orthodox kings as upheld Vedic rites and customs. The new kings of the post-Vedic ages seldom sought out the guidance of forest Rishis. So these forest Rishis gradually became either house-holder Brahmans seeking the patronage of kings in cities or forest anchorites cut off from the political and social life of cities. This important schism in the spiritual body which formed the very basis and regulative centre of Vedic culture and civilisation amounted in course of time to a cleft between the Gnanakanda and the Karmakanda, both of which aspects of Vedic wisdom the forest Rishi was supposed to combine in himself in the Vedic ages. As an inevitable consequence, rose on the one hand a blind Vedic orthodoxy exercising authority over Vedic society, and on the other a multiplication of monastic institutions covering a scattered array of numerous sects. Most of these monastic institutions seem to have become in course of time dissociated from an Upanishadic foundation, while a small number probably maintained the authority of the Vedas and carried on in its purest form the tradition of the Advaitic basis of Vedic ritualism.

19. Thus in the post-Vedic ages, the development of the inherited culture of the Vedas went on broadly from two centres—the society and the forest—the former being concerned with the Samhitas and the Brahmanas, the ritualistic or Karmakanda portion of the Srutis, and the latter with the Upanishads and the Sutras, the Gnanakanda portion of the Srutis. Thus, as time went on, the two parts of the Vedas got distinctly separated, so much so that the word Veda became synonymous with Vedic ritual, while among the monastics it became quite out of vogue to appeal to Vedic ritualistic authority. The spirit of the entire Vedic religion became smothered under a complicated mass of ritual—viewed by the

Atyasrami as useless pretensions to Vedic authority, because he had to live and work quite out of all touch with the Vedic orthodoxy, to which alone such pretensions would have counted—and the very meaning of the Vedic hymns had probably been forgotten, while the Brahman priests who lived in society were busying themselves with outward forms and ceremonies. A great gulf yawned between the masses and their spiritual leaders. A keen and persistent demand was arising from the many new evolving communities all over India foi religious dispensations to come out of the forest. These spreading and multiplying communities, the products of a social amalgamation that was going on all over the country, (vide Chapter II) Vedic orthodoxy was powerless to keep under control. Confronted with the phenomenon of a universal social revolution, Vedic orthodoxy, like a tortoise at the sight of danger, withdrew its powers of assimilation and amalgamation based on an Upanishadic foundation, into the shell of social restrictions. This stringent social policy left a large majority of the people outside the fold of Vedic orthodoxy. And a considerable section of this majority offered a large and a ready field for the spiritual ministrations of monastic sects like those of Jainism and Buddhism.

CHAPTER IV.

Mahavira and Gautama.

20. Such being the condition of India about 700 B. C., even when the social and religious state of the Hindus appeared to be on the throes of a mighty revolution, the dawn of a reformation was at hand. The advent of two Mahapurushas, Mahavira and Gautama, saved the situation.

21. Mahavira :—Born at Vaisali in Behar, Mahavira, a king's son, retired from the world in early manhood to lead a life of religious meditation. After some years of abstinence and profound study, light came to him, and he went forth to proclaim his discovery to the world. He thenceforth called himself a Jina or "conqueror" and in the course of a long life of itinerancy, gathered round him a numerous band of devoted disciples whom he organised into a monastic order

22. Gautama :—In or about 624 B. C., on the full moon day of the lunar month of Vaisakham, was born Gautama the Buddha at Kapilavastu of a regal family. The royal youth was much given to study and contemplation in spite of the attempts of his father to make him live an indifferent worldly life. His serious mind was impressed with the vanity of earthly gains and hopes, and his sympathetic nature was deeply stirred on behalf of the masses ground down under the spiritual exclusiveness of the Brahmans. He saw that what passed for religion was a mere empty observance of forms and ceremonies and so he determined to forsake his luxurious life and devote himself to the work of consoling and elevating mankind.

23. Gautama becomes Buddha :— After years of meditation in deep solitude enlightenment came upon him ; here are his words :—

"Long have I wandered ! Long !
Bound by the chain of desire

Through many births,
Seeking thus long in vain,
Whence comes this restlessness in man?
Whence his egotism, his anguish ?
And hard to bear is Samsara
When pain and death encompass us.
Found! It is found !
Author of selfhood,
No longer shalt thou build a house
for me.
Broken are the beams of sin ;
The ridgepole of care is shattered,
Into Nirvana my mind has passed,
The end of cravings has been reached
at last."

24. **Buddha's teachings** :—Buddha taught that salvation is within the reach of all, high and low alike; that he who leads a pure life and helps his fellow-creatures has no need to offer sacrifices to the gods; and that a man's present state is the result of his own acts in the present or in a past life. The aim of man should be to escape from the wheel of birth and death, to attain Nirvana,

not through vedic sacrifices nor through Brahman mediation, but by virtuous living, kindness to living beings and the suppression of passions.

25. Buddhism and Jainism compared :—Both the Buddhist and the Jainese systems relied on the support of an organised society of monks, and taught with insistence the doctrine of extreme respect for every form of life.

26. Jainese conquests :—Jainism never attempted any distant conquests. Although it became powerful in the south as well as in the north for several centuries, it never spread beyond the limits of India. The Jains are now mostly found in western India and Rajputana.

27. The secret of Buddha's success :—The two faiths were exclusively monastic, bearing close affinity and likeness to the many monastic faiths which evolved out of the Yoga and Sankhya philosophies. Buddha never displayed any antagonism to the Brahmans. He never deliberately set about to found a new religion. He was probably a social reformer and a great thinker on religion, who wished to solve the problem of human misery and alleviate it. He found the solution only in Nirvana and he proclaimed his truth. He was deeply learned in the Vedic philosophy, the philosophy of the Upanishads, and almost all he taught was borrowed from that philosophy. He preached in the language of the day, Pali, and boldly announced that all men might obtain salvation by charity and holy living. Herein lay the secret of his success. Prince and peasant, Brahman and Sudra, Aryan and non-Aryan, flocked alike to hear his message. But neither Mahavira nor Gautama sought to abolish caste.

28. The decline of Buddhism :— The Brahmans, those who lived in society, regarded Buddha as a mere social reformer, and interfered very little with his teaching. But, after Buddha's death, the ardent personal devotion of his disciples practically made Buddha a god instead of a moralist and a philosopher. The ritualistic Brahmans came in time to regard Buddha as an avatara who sought to delude demons with false doctrines. The people themselves had long been accustomed to look up to the Brahmans for spiritual knowledge. The growth of wealth in the monasteries was followed by corruptions in the Sangha, which lessened popular respect for the Buddhist teachers. Had not Buddha broken in upon society, Buddhism would have decidedly and easily fallen into line with the many ramifications of monastic religion developed from the Yoga and the Sankhya systems. But, unlike all these forest faiths which might be called its prototypes, Buddhism, an ideal religion of meditation, the object of which was the destruction of desire, not within the actual scope of those who heard its gospel, stepped out of its forest seclusion which was the cause alike of its success and of its fall. Although certain kings favoured and certain others persecuted Buddhism, the influence of the

Brahmans on the masses of the people was never completely lost. The Mussalman conquest in the 12th century tended to merge Buddhism into Brahmanism in the opposition that the Mahamadans offered to both. It is, however, curious to note that though Jainism never attained the popularity of Buddhism, the followers of Mahavira are still to be found in small communities all over India, and the Buddhists have practically disappeared from the country. The few who call themselves Buddhists at the present time base their faith upon foreign expositions of Buddhism made in the XIX and XX centuries.

———

CHAPTER V.

Foreign Invasions into India.

29. India is rather a continent than a country, so vast is its area (1,800,258 square miles) and so varied are the people inhabiting it. Within its boundaries dwells to day a population of over 315,000,000 (175 per square mile) speaking different languages.

30. India's attractions :—It may be said that till about the 4th century B. C., India was entirely and distinctly Aryan. The country was then as now full of broad rivers, high mountains, extensive and fertile plains, inhabited by one of the most highly civilised races of mankind. This ripe mango was hanging down from the great tree of the central Asiatic steppes,—a source of temptation to the various barbarous and semi-barbarous, greedy, envious people who lived in distant lands. But the double fortress-wall of the mighty Himalayas and the deep ocean-moat surrounding India on all sides prevented these foreigners from entering into the country. But the sluice-gates of the passes in the northwest, caused by some of the broad Indian rivers, were soon discovered; they were lifted again and again, letting the floods of foreign invasion descend upon the plains of India

31. Persian exploration :—About 500 B. C., King Darius of Persia sent an expedition to explore the Panjab. It is said that the land of the five rivers became a Persian province, to which it yielded a large revenue. Indian archers were probably included in the Persian army defeated at Plataea in Greece in 479 B. C. But how long the Persians ruled the Indus region and how and when they lost control of it is not known.

CHAPTER VI.

Alexander the Great.

32. Alexander, king of Macedon, had, during 334 to 331 B. C., conquered Egypt and all western Asia, defeating the Persian monarch in three pitched battles. In 326 B. C. he crossed the Indus, the then boundary between Persia and India. The king of Taxila submitted; but Porus, the raja of the country between the Indus and the Jhilum, tried to stop the invader. In the battle of the Hydaspes, the son of Porus was killed and Porus himself capitulated. However, Alexander restored his kingdom to him and treated him with the honour due to his rank. The victorious conqueror then passed eastward, receiving on the march the submission of the ruler of Kashmir. But the Kathaians who occupied the land between the Chenab and the Bias offered a stubborn resistance, but surrendered when their capital Sangala was captured and rased to the ground.

Magadha now lay before him, the kingdom he longed to conquer for the sake of its wealth. His war-worn veterans were, however, unwilling to proceed beyond the Bias, and so Alexander reluctantly gave orders for a retreat.

On his way back, he met with considerable opposition from the people of the land, and was himself severely wounded in the capture and assault of Multan. Near the junction of the five rivers he halted for a while and began the construction of a city which he named Alexandria. Then marching on to where the Indus branches out into its delta he founded another city, Pattala, which survives to this day. After suffering great hardships, he reached Persia in 325 B. C. In June 323, he died at Babylon at the early age of 32. He is known in history as the first great conqueror of the world.

33. Alexander's empire broken up :—No other man in the history of the world ever accomplished so much in so short a time and at such an early age. He had intended to annex the Punjab and Sindh to his empire, but his premature death made the task impossible—no other hand could wield the sceptre of universal dominion. The empire fell to pieces and was carved into kingdoms by his generals, none of whom was strong enough to hold the distant Indian provinces. In three or four years all traces of Macedonian rule in the Indus valley vanished. The Macedonian invasion had practically no effect on Indian institutions, except that it brought into contact with each other two most highly civilised nations of the ancient world. The Hindus probably felt Greek influence in science and art, while the Greeks must have imbibed something of the deep religious and philosophical speculations of the Hindus.

34. Selucus :—After Alexander's death, his vast empire broke up, and in the scramble which ensued, Selucus, one of his generals, seized Bactria and established an independent Greek kingdom.

After consolidating his power, he invaded India thinking to carry out the plans of conquest of Alexander.

CHAPTER VII.

Pre-Asokan Magadha.

35. The kingdom of Magadha attained the rank of a paramount power under king Jarasandha. The earliest capital was the hill-fort of Rajagriha. The most ancient king who can be approximately dated was Sisunaga (about 600 B. C.)

36. Bimbisara :—Bimbisara, the fifth Saisunaga king, founded a new capital at the base of the hill on which stood the old capital. He also annexed the small kingdom of Anga to the east. This annexation was the first step in Magadha's progress to greatness during historical times. Bimbasara was after a reign of 28 years starved to death by his son Ajatasatru. This king built a fort at Patali to check the incursions of his neighbours from Vaisali, which developed into the magnificent city of Pataliputra, the modern Patna.

It was during the reign of Bimbisara or Ajatasatru, that Darius, king of Persia sent an expedition to explore the Punjab. Thus the Indus valley became a province of the Persian empire. But how or when the Persians lost control of this province is not known (Vide Chapter V.)

37. Mahapadma Nanda :— When Mahapadma Nanda, the son of the last Saisunaga king by a sudra woman, was reigning, Alexander the great invaded India. The latter had heard of the vast wealth of the kingdom of Magadha, and of the unpopularity of it's king.

38. Chandragupta Maurya :—After Alexander's death and before Selucus invaded India, Chandragupta Maurya, an exiled prince from the court of Nanda, had actually succeeded in carrying out, aided by Chanakya a clever Brahman, the project which he had proposed he and Alexander should jointly effect. He had since entered upon a career of conquest and at the time of the invasion of Selucus had extended his sway over the whole of northern India. He seems to have been the first supreme ruler of Hindustan within historical times, his dominions extending from the Bay of Bengal to the Arabian sea, and reaching southwards probably as far as the Narbada.

39. Selucus :—About 305 B. C. Selucus crossed the Indus. But Chandragupta was too strong for him. Selucus was therefore obliged to give up all thought of conquest in India and to surrender some of his provinces west of the Indus. Thus the Hindu Kush mountains became the frontier of the Indian empire. Chandragupta, however, like the true Hindu that he was, gave Selucus 500 elephants, married his daughter and received a Greek ambassador at his court.

40. Magasthanes:—This ambassdor, Magasthanes, lived at Pataliputra for a long time and spent his leisure in compiling a careful account of the geography, products and institution of India. The book has been lost, but extracts from it have been preserved by other writers.

His statements disclose a well-ordered state, governed by a stern, capable despot, who did not hesitate to shed blood, and consequently lived in daily fear of assassination.

The capital, a city 10 miles long and 2 miles broad, protected on one side by the Ganges, and on the other by a deep ditch, surrounded on all sides by a wooden wall, was administered by a municipal commission composed of six panchayats. The other great cities of the empire were probably governed on similar lines. The empire was a loose confederacy of 118 towns, under the suzerainty of the ruler of Pataliputra, but practically independent in matters of internal administration. The general administrative machinery consisted of six boards, four for the four kinds of army, one for transport, commissariat and field service, and the sixth for admiralty affairs.

There was a vast standing army of 9,000 elephants attended by 36,000 men, 30,000 cavalry and 600,000 infantry. Chandragupta's chariots numbered probably more than 8,000.

Elaborate rules providing for the treatment of strangers show that the empire had constant dealings with foreign states.

Irrigation was carefully attended to by a special department, Many taxes and cesses besides land revenue and water rates were levied. Cultivators were exempt from military service. The people had simple and frugal habits, but possessed an extravagant love of ornament and show. The revenue and penal codes were severe and sternly administered. Theft, wilful false statements, and other crimes were punished by mutilation. Evasion of the duty on goods sold was punishable with death. Judicial torture, of which there were 18 kinds, including 7 varieties of whipping, for exacting confessions was recognised and freely used. A regular system of excise was also in force.

The people required no locks to their doors; above all no Indian was ever known to tell a lie. The Hindus scarcely ever had recourse to a law-suit; and they lived peaceably.

Buddhism had probably been deprived of royal favour and dwindled into insignificance.

41. Asoka's accession :—Chandragupta died in 297 B. C., and was succeeded by his son Bindusara. He reigned for 28 years and extended his father's empire by fresh conquests. He was succeeded by his renowned son Asokavardhana in 272 B. C.

CHAPTER VIII.

Asoka (272 to 232 B. C.).

42. Asoka, the governor of Ujjain at the time of his father's death, succeeded to the throne after a fierce fratricidal struggle. His coronation took place four years after. (269 B. C.)

43. The extent of Asoka's empire :—The early years of his reign were spent in extending the empire of Magadha by adding to it the territory of the Kalingas, the country on the coast of the Bay of Bengal between the Mahanadi and the Godavari rivers. Under him, the empire of Magadha became the greatest that had up to then been known in India.

In the northwest, his empire extended to the Hindu Kush and included Afghanistan, Baluchistan and Sindh. In the north, the empire included the districts round Srinagar, which city Asoka built, and south-east Nepal, where he built another city Bengal and Kalinga acknowledged his sway. The Deccan had already been conquered by Chandragupta or Bindusara. The Andhra kingdom between the Godavari and the Krishna rivers seems to have been a protected state. The southern frontier probably coincided with the 13th degree of latitude. The Tamil kingdoms of Chola, Chera and Pandya in the extreme south seem, however, to have remained independent.

44. **Dharmasoka** :—During the war with Kalinga, Asoka was horrified at the suffering caused by his ambition. Buddhist chronicles say that he was notorious in his early days for violence and cruelty. But the miseries inflicted by an aggressive war upon a prosperous and civilised people worked so much upon his mind that they altered the whole tenour of his life. "His Majesty felt profound sorrow and regret at the slaughter, death and captivity of the people"—Asoka is reported to have spoken.

His first war was his last, and Chandasoka became Dharmasoka.

45. Buddhist propaganda work :- About 258 B. C. Asoka became a Buddhist. His ardent nature and his firm faith in the mild and gentle creed of Buddha made him do all in his power to guide mankind along it. Buddhism became the state religion and its doctrines were proclaimed far and wide.

46. Buddhist Council :—About 256 B. C. he convened at his capital a council of Buddhist monks (the first great religious council) to settle the faith and classify and compile the Buddhist scriptures.

47. Edicts :—In the same year, he issued edicts setting forth the tenets of the faith and had them inscribed on rocks and stone pillars in different parts of the kingdom. These records exist to this day at Orissa, Mysore, the Punjab, the Bombay coast and other places.

One of the inscriptions on a rock

in Mysore reads: "Thus says His Majesty: 'Father and mother must be obeyed; respect for living creatures must be enforced; truth must be spoken. These are the virtues of the law of Dharma which must be practised. The teacher must be revered by the pupil and proper courtesy must be shown to relations. This is the ancient standard of piety—this leads to length of days—and according to this men must act.'"

48. Asoka's Seva:—In all these edicts the king styles himself "देवानां प्रियदर्शि"—beloved of the gods. He ordered the faithful in each district to gather once in every five years for religious instruction. He appointed Buddhist ministers to go into every land to attend to the spiritual needs of the believers and to teach those who had not yet heard the Law. He enjoined universal religious toleration and exhorted his subjects to be ever extolling virtue and imparting true religion to one another. He prohibited the slaughter of animals for food or sacrifice. He provided medicines for man and beast in all the realms over which he exercised suzerainty, dug wells and built rest-houses along the public roads, and planted medicinal herbs, fruit trees and trees to afford shade to travellers wherever they were needed.

49. Missionary organisation :— Buddhist monasteries enjoyed the special patronage of the state. Asoka's son Mahendra and his daughter Sanghamitra became Bhikshus and went to Ceylon as missionaries to spread the faith. Soon the king of Ceylon became a Buddhist and erected a stately monastery for those who joined the order, and there the brother and sister lived and taught for the rest of their lives.

The emperor organised a system of foreign missions to carry his teaching to all the states on the frontiers of his empire including the Himalayan regions (Kashmir, Afghanistan, Lower Burma and Indo-China), to the independent Tamil kingdoms of the far south and Ceylon, and to the Greek monarchies of Bactria, Syria, Egypt, Cyrene, Macedonia and Epirus, thus embracing three continents, Asia, Europe and Africa. Everything that could be done was done to spread the religion of Buddha and insure obedience to its tenets, short of persecution or forcible conversion.

It must be distinctly remembered that though Asokavardhana did so much to spread Buddhism, the followers of other religions were not persecuted. He followed the policy of a strict and impartial religious neutrality in the political administration of the country, a policy so essential to success, and Asoka realised it to the fullest extent.

50. Asoka's greatness :—In this way, Buddhism, which had merely been the creed of a local Indian sect of reformers, became one of the chief religions of the world ; and today it counts millions of Chinese, Japanese and several others among its votaries. This result is the work of Asoka alone, and entitles him to rank for all time to come in that small body of men who have changed the faiths of the world.

In about 232 B. C. the great Asoka-vardhana passed away after having reigned for 41 years. He had been strong enough to keep in check the whole extent of his vast empire and had preserved friendly relations with the independent kingdoms on its borders. Few kings have been so earnest and noble-minded as Asoka and have exercised a greater influence for good upon mankind.

CHAPTER IX.

The Sunga dynasty.

51. After Asoka's death, his empire broke up and his descendants seem to have retained only Magadha and the neighbouring provinces. Nothing is known about their reigns. These princes seem to have enjoyed only limited power and to have been incapable of holding the empire together, once the controlling hand of Asoka was removed. The last of the Mauryas, Brihadratha, was slain in or about 184 B. C. by his commander-in-chief Pushyamitra Sunga who seized the throne.

52. Pushyamitra Sunga :— This Pushyamitra is said to have been a staunch supporter of Brahmanism; and in his time, perhaps owing to religious differences, the outlying provinces of the empire revolted and formed themselves into independent kingdoms.

53. The break-up of the empire :- Very little is on record about the Sunga dynasty founded by Pushyamitra which is said to have lasted for 112 years. (184 to 72 B. C.) The great grammarian Patanjali was a contemporary of Pushyamitra, in whose reign, (155 B. C.) the Greek king Menander invaded India. The Bactrian Greeks led by their brilliant king-commander seized upon Afghanistan and the Punjab, conquered Sindh, Guzerat and Malwa, and penetrated as far as Saketa in Kosala. The empire of Magadha about this time began to decline rapidly, and within a short time lost all its provinces. Kalinga and Andhra were the first to regain their independence.

The various causes that led to the decline of the Magadha empire may be attributed to (1) the vastness of the empire; it is not any and every ruler that can rule mighty empires with success; after Alexander's death his empire fell; after Asoka's death his empire fell; (2) the absence of political unity among the various component parts of the empire and the spirit of revolt in the smaller kingdoms for independent domination ; (3) the comparative weakness of the later rulers ; and (4) the numerous foreign invasions referred to in Chapter XI.

54. The Kanwa dynasty :—The Sungas were succeeded by the Kanwa dynasty by about 72 B. C. The last Sunga was killed by an Andhra prince in about 27 B. C. But the Andhras had become independent some two centuries earlier, probably soon after the death of Asoka.

CHAPTER X.

The Andhras.

55. The Andhra nation occupied in Chandragupta's time the deltas of the Godavari and the Krishna. After Asoka's death, the Andhras rapidly extended their power to the sources of the Godavari and soon stretched right across the peninsula from the Arabian sea to the bay of Bengal. About 145 A. D. Sourashtra, Malwa, Cutch, Sindh and the Konkan became independent of Andhra control. The Andhras had also become unable to push their conquests south of the Krishna, and the Cholas, the Cheras and the Pandyas maintained their ancient sway.

The Andhra kings were Buddhists, but their history is extremely obscure. There is no distinct evidence that they held Magadha.*

---

* In the Bellary district has recently been discovered an inscription relating to an Andhra king who reigned about A. D. 135. The inscription is important as it includes Bellary in the Andhra dominions of the time.

56. The Chalukyas :—When the Andhra power declined in the Deccan, the Chalukyas rose into power. Their most notable king Pulikesin II (608 to 642 A. D.) successfully withstood the invasion of his dominions by Harsha. His capital at or near Nasik was visited by Hiuen Tsang the Chinese Buddhist pilgrim in A. D. 641.

CHAPTER XI.

Foreign Invasions.

57. The Scythians :—About the middle of the 2nd century B. C. the nomad and pastoral tribes of central Asia called the Scythians or Sakas overwhelmed the Greek kingdom of Bactria and set up governments of their own. They made their way into India and, having subdued Afghanistan and Kashmir, turned their steps into the Punjab and soon established themselves in Sindh and Saurashtra. By the beginning of the last century B. C., they had become the paramount power in northern India and ruled over a territory as far south as the Vindhya hills. But under the influence of Grecian and Indian culture, they had changed from wandering savages into a settled and civilised people. They formed themselves into a loose confederacy governed by provincial administrators called satraps (क्षत्रप). In B. C. 57, they suffered a crushing defeat at the hands of the people of Malwa who rose in rebellion against them. And in the first century A. D. they were attacked by the Parthians from the north who wrested from them the northern part of their dominions.

58. The Yueh-Chi :—Another nomad tribe from central Asia, the Yueh-Chi, descended through Bactria and Kabul into India and seized the Punjab and Kashmir. The Sakas prevented them, however, from taking Guzerat, where they established a powerful and independent kingdom. The Saka era, 78 A. D., marks the date of this declaration of independence. In later ages, this era came to be known as that of Salivahana, while the year of the Sakas' defeat at the hands of the people of Malwa, 57 B. C., came to be known as the Vikrama era.

59. The Kusanas :—The Kusana branch of the Yueh-Chi, which had played a prominent part in humbling the Parthians, extended its dominions rapidly. About the middle of the first century A. D.,

Kadphises, a Kusana chief, conquered the various Greek and Parthian princes on the frontier and made himself master of a large part of northwest India, where his coins are still found abundantly.

60. Kanishka :—His successor was Kanishka who came to the throne in about 120 A. D. His capital was Purushapura (Peshawar), from which he ruled Kabul, Kashmir and all northern India, perhaps as far as the Narbada. His empire towards the west reached the Persian frontier.

61. Buddhism under Kanishka :—He was a zealous Buddhist and like Asoka he summoned a council of Buddhist monks to prepare authorised commentaries on the scriptures. This council settled the creed of the northern Buddhists (Mahayana) as Asoka's had settled that of the southern (Hinayana). It was in Kanishka's reign that Buddhist missionaries were sent northwards into Tibet and China.

62. Kanishka's successors:—After

his death, his son Suvishka succeeded to the sole government of the whole empire.

In the reign of his successor Vasudeva, the empire began to break up. Scarely anything is known about the history of northern India from this time to the rise of the Gupta dynasty in A. D. 320.

Kanishka and his son spent much money on Buddhist monasteries and sthupas at Mathura, Peshawar and other places, traces of which still exist. The medical author Charaka is reputed to have lived in Kanishka's time.

63. Rudrasena :—The Saka kingdom of Guzerat (Saurashtra) meanwhile grew and prospered. Its kings, known as the western satraps, were Hindus by religion. Nahapana who ascended the throne in 119 A. D. paid extravagant honours to Brahmans: But his kingdom was invaded by the Andhra Buddhist king Gautamiputra who slew Nahapana. The latter's heir, Chasthana, was however, able enough to conquer Malwa; and Rudrasena, a later king, by extensive conquests, made himself the most powerful king of India and twice the Andhra raja was defeated at his hands. This Rudrasena was probably a contemporary of Samudra Gupta.

In the beginning of the third century A. D., the Kusana and the Andhra dynasties grew less powerful and their empires were broken up into minor states.

CHAPTER XII.

The Guptas.

64. The break-up of these kingdoms favoured the rise of daring and skilful adventurers. A man of the name of Gupta, probably a foreigner, succeeded in restoring Pataliputra to its ancient glories. His son and grandson continued the work of extension and consolidation. The latter, Chandra Gupta I, enhanced his power at the beginning of the fourth century A. D. by marrying a princess and formed a considerable kingdom extending along the Ganges to Allahabad. In 320 A. D. he established the Gupta era to commemorate his coronation.

65. Samudra Gupta :—The greatest of the Guptas was, however, Samudra Gupta, and under him the kingdom grew into a mighty empire. He stands forth as a real man—scholar, poet, musician and warrior. The early years of his reign were devoted to the thorough conquest of upper India. His dominions extended from the Hooghli to the Jumna and from the Himalayas to the Narbada. The Ganges delta, Assam and northern Rajputana were under his protection.

66. Samudra Gupta's South Indian Campaign :—He organised a great south Indian campaign, but achieved no permanent conquest. He marched through the valleys of the Mahanadi to the wild forests of Orissa, took two hillforts in Ganjam, conquered Pithapuram and defeated the Pallava kings of Kanchi and Palghat. Returning through the western parts of the Deccan, he subdued Devarashtra and Khandesh He was simply content with receiving the humble submission of the vanquished princes and bringing home a large store of golden bounty. He celebrated the Asvamedha and bestowed large gifts on the Brahmans.

67. The Allahabad Pillar :—The elegant inscriptions on a stone pillar still standing at Allahabad record the conquests of Samudra Gupta and speak also of his personal qualities. The evidence as to his musical skill is confirmed by the medals which exhibit the king in the act of playing the vina.

68. Chandra Gupta II :—His son and successor Chandra Gupta II, surnamed Vikramaditya, annexed Malwa and Ujjain to his empire. He dispossessed the Saka rulers of Saurashtra in 409 A. D. He seems to have made Ayodhya his capital. He reigned from about 375 to 413 A. D.

CHAPTER XIII.

Chinese pilgrims:—Fa Hian.

69. During the reign of Chandra Gupta II, about 399 A. D., Fa Hian, a Chinese Buddhist, came to India on a pilgrimage. He remained for six years in the dominions of Chandra Gupta studying Buddhist literature and was much pleased with the country. Although the Gupta king was himself a Hindu, Buddhism flourished and was fully tolerated. The country was filled with monasteries. Buddhist monks were everywhere supported without stint, but Hindu temples also had their votaries, and in every large town, Hindu temples and Buddhist monasteries flourished side by side.

70. The pilgrim's travels:—The pilgrim found Pataliputra a flourishing city with numerous charitable institutions and a free hospital. Asoka's palace was in ruins, but close at hand was a handsome monastery with six or seven hundred monks. In Malwa the penal code was mild and the people were not worried by official regulations. Order was well preserved and the pilgrim was free to pursue his studies in peace. Sravasti, a flourishing city in Buddha's time, was almost deserted. Kapilavastu, the birthplace of Buddha, was a scene of desolation. Kusinagara where Buddha died was inhabited only by a few priests and their families.

Fa Hian also visited Rajagriha where he saw the cave in which Asoka's Buddhist council was held. Gaya he found a wilderness. Benares, the stronghold of the Hindus to this day, where Buddha first preached his sermon, had only two monasteries, but many Hindu temples. Throughout northern India, no copy of the Buddhist scriptures could be found, and the Bhikshus only relied on tradition for their knowledge of the precepts. At Pataliputra he at last procured copies of Buddhist scriptures. He returned to China by sea.

71. Condition of Buddhism :—But the Buddhism that Fa Hian saw was very different from the Buddhism of Asoka. Gorgeous festivals, quite opposed to the spirit of ancient Hinduism and Buddhism, had become recognised institutions, and the Buddhists had taken to a universal idolatrous worship of Buddha. Fa Hian is also said to have witnessed a huge procession of 20 four-wheeled cars surmounted with gaudy imitation pagodas dragged through the streets amid shouting crowds. At the four corners of each car were images of Buddha in a sitting posture, and round the pagodas, under embroidered canopies, figures of the gods adorned with ornaments of gold, silver and glass.

To such idolatrous pomp had the pure and simple faith of Buddha degenerated by the fifth century A. D., probably owing to the influx of outlandish manners and customs seeking to be infused into the views of the old life of India, through the channels cut by the missionary zeal of the Buddhists; and the result was the slow sinking of the country in the dusky waters of the anomaly of faith and acharas.

CHAPTER XIV.

The later Guptas.

72. Chandra Gupta II was succeeded by his son Kumara Gupta who reigned from 413 to 455 A. D. During his reign a fresh horde of Central Asian nomads, the white Huns, invaded India.

73. The White Hun Invasion :— The Huns, a Mongol tribe, moved westwards from the steppes of Central Asia in the second half of the 4th century A. D. to seek subsistence for their growing numbers. Led by Attila, they laid the Roman empire under tribute. But after Attila's death in 453 A. D. the white Huns were signally defeated and driven out of Europe. Then they turned upon India under their general Toraman. They overcame Skanda Gupta, the next Gupta king, by about 480 A. D. By the beginning of the 6th century the Gupta kingdom had suffered so much from the ravages of these barbarians that it was reduced to insignificance and soon after disappeared from history.

74. The break-up of the Gupta empire :—One after another, the outlying provinces of the Gupta empire fell into their hands. Toraman died in 515 A. D. and his son Mihiragula proved even a greater scourge than his father. Wherever this ruthless and savage warrior went, he left behind him scenes of ruin and desolation to mark his victorious course. But by about 528 A. D. he was defeated by a confederacy of Hindu princes led by Yasodharman, raja of Malwa, and forced to retire into Kashmir.

75. Vikramaditya :—Efforts have been made to identify this Yasodharman with the famous Vikramaditya of Sanskrit literature. It is not the less probable that Chandra Gupta II, successor of Samudra Gupta, surnamed Vikramaditya, who conquered Ujjain in about 390 A. D., may be identical with the hero Vikramaditya of Sanskrit literary fame. This Vikramaditya is said to have gathered round him nine pre-eminent men of letters, *navaratna*, amongst whom were Kalidasa the poet and dramatist, Dhanvantari the physician, Varahamihira the astronomer, Amarasimha the lexicographer, Bhetala Bhatta the politician, Vararuchi the grammarian, and other great and learned men. Popular belief associates the Vikrama era with 56 B. C.

76. The Gupta period the Golden age of India :—It should be said here that the Gupta period is the golden age of India. Powerful and long-lived kings, themselves scholars, governed the country well. Great and learned men like Kalidasa of the immortal Sakuntala fame were duly honoured. The Allahabad pillar shows us their architectural taste. Sciences, music, etc., had also reached a high state of efficiency. There was no religious persecution.

The Guptas were zealous Hindus; and during their time, Sanskrit learning revived, and Buddhism began markedly to decline.

CHAPTER XV.

The Harsha empire.

77. After the death of Yasodharman, his kingdom must have rapidly declined, for very little is known of Malwa subsequently. The kings of Thaneswar (स्थानेश्वर,) Prabhakara and Rajyavardhana, who were engaged in fierce conflicts with the white Huns for nearly 50 years, threw off the yoke of Malwa and annexed Kanouj.

78. Rajyavardhana :—Rajyavardhana a staunch Buddhist marched against Sasanka the king of western Bengal, who had been persecuting the Buddhists and had actually cut the famous Bo-tree at Gaya, and defeated him. But Sasanka treacherously murdered Rajyavardhana. Harshavardhana, a younger brother of Rajyavardhana, marched into Bengal and destroyed the kingdom.

79. Harshavardhana :—Harshavardhana ascended the throne of Thaneswar in A. D. 606. He was a great conqueror and by 612 made himself the master of northern India including Nepal, Saurashtra, Guzerat, Assam and Bengal. He removed his capital to Kanouj, a more fitting site for the metropolis of a great empire.

80. Pulikesin II :—The equally vigourous ruler of the Deccan, Pulikesin II, the greatest of the Chalukya dynasty, (608 to 642 A. D.) prevented him from extending his dominions south of the Narbada, as stated in Chapter X supra.

81. The break-up of the empire :- Harsha was a great king and encouraged learning. Bana, one of the greatest of Indian poets, flourished at his court. He himself is the author of the Sanskrit drama Ratnavali. His display of religious zeal was excessive and he squandered the resources of the state upon it. When he died in 647 A. D., his treasury was empty and his empire quickly fell to pieces. Within a hundred years, a king of Kashmir, Lalitaditya, sacked Kanouj and carried off with him as part of the spoils of war the poet Bhavabhuti who was then living at the court of Kanouj.

82. The Chalukya dynasty :—The Chalukya dynasty, referred to in § 80 above, rose into importance in the middle of the 6th century A. D., when the Andhra power declined (vide Chapter X). The Chalukyas drove the Pallavas from their homes between the Godavari and the Krishna and rapidly extended their empire.

83. Northern India after the Harshas :—By this time, Kalinga had been depopulated and was covered with jungle. Sindh and the Punjab had also become independent kingdoms. With the fall of the Harsha empire, the history of northern India practically ceases for 200 years.

CHAPTER XVI.

Hiuen Tsang or Yuan Chung.

84. Hiuen Tsang was a Chinese pilgrim who came to India in 629 A. D. and stayed in the country till 645 A. D. He visited almost every part of India. He became a personal friend of King Harsha, who in his later days took a fancy to Buddhism. The king was a vigourous despot keeping his dominions in order by personal supervision exercised during constant touring. The penal code was rather more severe than in the days of the Guptas and the roads were not quite so safe, but the country seems to have been fairly well governed.

85. The pilgrim's travels :— In Afghanistan, through which the Chinaman entered India, he found that Buddhism had degenerated into idolatry. Many of the monasteries were deserted. In Kashmir the two religions, Brahmanism and Buddhism, were flourishing side by side. In

Mathura, Buddhism had a strong following though great attention was paid to outward forms and ceremonies, a sign of deterioration. Kurukshetra and Hardvar were full of Hindu temples.

86. Harsha's capital :—The city of Kanouj was surrounded by solid walls and deep ditches and was noted for its wealth. The people were noble and gracious in appearance, famed for their learning and piety and noted for the purity of their speech. King Harsha, after the manner of Asoka, held quinquennial assemblies, forbade the killing of animals, provided hospitals and dispensaries throughout his kingdom and did a thousand other things of the same sort. Hiuen Tsang was often a spectator of magnificent processions in honour of Buddha, in which his image in gold was carried amid jewelled banners, embroidered umbrellas, clouds of incense and showers of flowers. The king scattered the wealth of his treasury broadcast among the people and feasted Buddhists and Brahmans indiscriminately. The idolatrous pomp exceeded even that referred to by Fa Hian. Brahmans and Buddhists often met to discuss the merits of the two faiths.

87. Benares :—Allahabad was entirely under Brahman influence. Sravasti, Kapilavastu and Kusinagara had been forsaken even by the monks. Near Benares, the seat of orthodox Hinduism to the present day, was a magnificent monastery 200 feet high possessing a noble image of Buddha in copper and inhabited by 1500 monks.

88. Magadha :—Buddhism still flourished in Magadha, but Pataliputra was in ruins, probably a result of the Hun incursions. Gaya was a Brahman colony, but the remnants of the Bodhi tree were surrounded by high brick walls and innumerable sthupas and images of Buddha. Near at hand was the stateliest and most beautiful of all the Buddhist monasteries; It was a monastery and a temple combined, a mass of ornamental work, in which had been lavished the utmost skill of the architect and the artist. It was built by a king of Ceylon and contained an image of Buddha in gold and silver adorned with precious stones.

89. Nalanda :—Close to Gaya was Nalanda, the most important of the Indian universities. The Nalanda vihara, the largest of its kind, capable of holding 10,000 monks, was established by a king of central India, and a long succession of kings continued the work of building, using all the skill of the sculptor till the whole was truly marvellous to behold. The lands in its possession contained more than 200 villages, these having been bestowed on the monastery by kings of many generations. In this university the teachers were men of conspicuous talent, solid learning, exalted eloquence and illustrious virtue, whose fame had spread through distant regions. From morning till night the teachers and pupils engaged in continuous discussion. Learned men from different cities went there in multitudes to settle their doubts, and the streams of wisdom and knowledge spread far and wide. Yuan Chung gives a detailed description of the course of studies at this university which included both religious and secular subjects. The pupils started with the study of the "Siddhavastu" and then they were instructed in the five chief vidyas, Sabdavidya the science of sounds, Silpavidya the science of mechanics, Chikitsavidya the science of medicine, Hetuvidya the science of causes and Adhyatmavidya the science of Brahman. The Brahmans also studied the four Vedas.

Yuan Chung was welcomed here on his arrival by 200 monks.

90. South India :—He then proceeded through Bengal to Orissa. Puri was a famous place of Buddhist pilgrimage. The kingdom of Berar was ruled by a Kshatriya king who honoured the laws of Buddha. Hiuen Tsang speaks of a rock-cut monastery there which was the wonder of all India. Kalinga had sunk into insignificance and the country of the Andhras had greatly declined in prosperity. Chola, one of the most important kingdoms in southern India, was mostly desolate and its cities were in ruins. Kanchi had beautiful buildings and its people were enlightened. Wherever he went, he saw hundreds of monasteries and thousands of priests. Pulikesin Chalukya, the ruler of Maharashtra, whose capital the pilgrim visited, had successfully withstood the all-conquering armies of Harsha and ruled over a people, impetuous in war, impulsive, proud and vindictive. In Malwa he found many monasteries and some 2,000 Buddhist priests. The people were renowned for their learning and politeness. The king of Guzerat, a close relation of Harsha, was a zealous Buddhist. The people were polite and learned, and had amassed great wealth in trade.

Wherever he went, he found that the people required no locks to their doors; above all, no Indian was ever known to tell a lie. The men scarcely ever had recourse to a law-suit and lived peaceably.

91. General :—In general, the Chinaman observed Buddhism on the wane. The faith had grown corrupt in the hands of illiterate priests. The majority of the clergy and the laity had forgotten the ethics of Buddha's teaching. The simple story of his life had been surrounded by legends and miraculous tales. Divine honours were paid to his relics. The monastic system had grown to unwieldy proportions. The monks had become wealthy and as a consequence were often found to lead idle, dissolute and avaricious lives. The evils of enforced celibacy upon all kinds of people, who sought admission into the monasteries, corrupted the priests, and as a result the people were left without guidance.

92. Absence of political unity :— Though the races of India were on the whole learned and polite, political unity seems to have been unknown among them. Such union as there was at any time was based upon the prowess of some great leader. Empires fell to pieces as soon as the reigning monarchy showed signs of weakness. The people were scarcely affected by a change of rule. This very lack of political life served to strengthen the bonds of religion and to preserve ancient customs and beliefs.*

93. Yuan Chung's return to China :—The pilgrim is said to have taken with him 657 volumes of manuscript which he had collected during his stay in India.

---

* The expression "political unity" is here used in the western sense of the term. In ancient India the village was the political unit and not the kingdom or the empire. There was always a strong and a vigourous village corporate life, which made the people too conservative and too indifferent to the political welfare of the country at large in preference to that of the village organisation.

CHAPTER XVII.

Rajput Ascendancy.

94. During the period immediately succeeding the fall of the Harsha empire, Buddhism had considerably declined and a new Hinduism had largely taken its place. This new Hinduism kept in some of the accretions of the Buddhistic age, only coloured here and there with the tint of the ancient faith. The huge temples seen in every nook and corner of the country today is the legacy which Buddhism has left behind; for after the disappearance of the religion of the Buddha, the simple fire-place-worship of the Brahmans had to a large extent to be substituted by places of public worship. This new Hinduism, the consequence of Buddhistic degeneracy, was largely supported by the Rajputs, the descendants of the ancient Kshatriyas.

95. Kumarila Bhatta:—The Hindu reaction against Buddhism was carried, further, early in the eighth century, by a Brahman Kumarila Bhatta who taught the Mimamsa philosophy and is popularly supposed to have led an active persecution of the Buddhists.

96. Sankaracharya :—While the Rajputs, the constitutional defenders of Hinduism, probably were expelling Buddhism by force, a champion of Hinduism arose in Southern India, who taught a form of Vedanta philosophy which indeed may be said to have swept Buddhism out of India. Sankaracharya, who was born in 788 A. D. in Malabar, was a profound Sanskrit scholar, a deep philosophical thinker and a great preacher.* During his short life of 32 years he wandered from place to place propounding his philosophy. His teachings spread throughout the length and breadth of India.

* One Mr. T. S. Narayana Sastriar, B.A., B.L., High Court Vakil, Madras, is just announcing his forthcoming publication "The Age of Sankara". He proposes to prove therein that Sankaracharya was born 13 centuries earlier, *i. e.*, in 509 B. C

97. The lasting effects of Buddhism on India:—Thus, though Sankara gave a tremendous impetus to the religious life of India, his philosophy could not recover her from the blow she received from Buddhism. Buddha's preaching of non-injury had been misunderstood as non-resistance even to wrongs inflicted. And in pursuance of this belief, the people sought to become passive, the consequence of which was the total extinction of the Kshatriya Dharma in India. As an example of this want of martial valour may be stated the recent "instance of a stupid Rajah of Tanjore" who, when his enemies surrounded his fort, ordered that the gates be thrown open and the way filled with sacred Tulasi. Said the valiant king, "Oh, if those mlecchas dare trample on my holy Tulasi, let them take my kingdom." Though we find some Kshatriya exploits here and there in the subsequent ages, as in the case of the Rajput opposition to Islam, yet, that martial spirit, that Kshatra Dharma. which had been so predominant in the heart of India, forming the most necessary constituent of her broadly planned social life, the Varnasrama Dharma, in the pre-Buddhistic ages, disappeared from the land for ever. Sankara revived the spiritually exalted Brahmanya Dharma, but he could not bring to life again the Kshatra Viryam, nor did he make any effort for that. Now these Kshatriyas were the defenders of the nation ; with their extinction, was opened a broad way for the unavoidable imposition on India of foreign rule during the last one thousand years and more.

CHAPTER XVIII.

Minor Hindu Kingdoms.*

98. Kanouj :—In A. D. 880, the most powerful state in northern India was that of Panchala or Kanouj, then ruled by Raja Bhoja Parihara. For 50 or 60 years after the middle of the 9th century, the kings of Kanouj governed a dominion rivalling that of Harsha in extent.

99. Bengal :—At the same time, the Pala kings were lords of Bengal and Bihar and enjoyed great power. They were often at war with Kanouj, and early in the 9th century, Dharmapala was strong enough to depose a king of Kanouj and replace him by another.

100. Jejakabhukti :—The Chandels of Bundelkhand (Jejakabhukti) had their capital at Mahola. Their kingdom was at the height of its grandeur in A. D. 1000.

---

* This chapter is necessarily incomplete.

101. Dhara :—Raja Bhoja of Dhara in Malwa who reigned from about A. D. 1018 to 1060 was a liberal patron of Sanskrit learning. It is perhaps this Bhoja who is the author of the celebrated Sanskrit work Bhojachampu.

102. The Chalukyas :—The Andhras held the Deccan till about 236 A. D. When their power declined, the Chalukyas rose into importance (vide Chapter XV). The latter established themselves at Vatapi or Nasik. Their most notable king was Pulikesin II (608 to 642 A. D.) who withstood the attacks of king Harshavardhana. The Chinese pilgrim Yuan Chung visited his capital in A. D. 641. The pilgrim has recorded that the people had a high and a warlike spirit. Though the king treated neighbouring countries with contempt, he prized learning and received loyal service from his subjects. The kingdom contained more than a hundred Buddhist monasteries with more than 5,000 monks; but votaries of Hindu gods were also numerous. In 642 A. D., Pulikesin Chalukya was humbled by the Pallavas of Kanchi, but the Chalukya dynasty lasted for about four centuries afterwards. In the end, it became merged in the Chola kingdom of the south. The best paintings in the caves of Ajanta date from the time of the first Chalukya dynasty in the 6th and 7th centuries A. D.

103. The Rashtrakutas :—In the middle of the 8th century, the Rashtra kutas possessed the sovereignty of the Deccan. Their kings acquired great power. Amoghavarsha, a Jain, who reigned in the 9th century for nearly 60 years, was reckoned by the Mahamadan writers of the 9th and 10th centuries to be one of the four great kings of the world, the other three being the Khalif of Bagdad, the emperor of China and the Sultan of Constantinople. Rashtrakuta Krishna I, in the latter half of the 8th century, had the marvellous rock-cut Kailasa temple at Ellora executed. In 916 A. D. the Rashtrakutas captured Kanouj, but in 973 A. D. they gave way before the Chalukyas.

104. Mysore :—At the close of the 13th century, Mysore was held by the Hoysala or Bellal dynasty. The Hoysala capital Dwarasamudra was captured by Malik Kafur in 1310 and reduced to ruins by Mahamad Bin Taghlak in 1327. The conversion of the Hoysala king Bittiga in the 12th century from Jainism to Vaishnavaism marks the influence of the great religious preacher Sri Ramanuja. The Hoysala kings of Mysore erected in the 12th and 13th centuries many magnificent Hindu temples.

105. The Yadavas :—The western side of the Deccan (Maharashtra ?) was in the 13th century under the rule of the Yadavas. Ramachandra the Yadava king had to submit to Ala-ud-din and then to Malik Kafur. His son Harapala tried to shake off the foreign yoke, but was defeated in 1318 by Mubarak who caused him to be flayed alive.

106. The Cholas :—In the 10th and 11th centuries, the Chola kingdom under Rajaraja and his successors became the leading power in the south and maintained a strong fleet. The Cholas are said to have carried on considerable trade even with the Roman empire and to have held the kingdom of Pegu under subjection. The Chola kings were zealous devotees of Siva and some of them are said to have cruelly persecuted the Jains. The great temple at Tanjore is said to have been built by the Cholas.

Many Chola epigraphs have been discovered in the North Arcot District. All the records invariably mention the "Assembly" and its activities. The "Assembly" consisted of both the young and the old of the village. It had its own halls, built sometimes by the king and sometimes by other benefactors, where it met and transacted the business of the village. One of the committees under its control was in charge of general village affairs and another in charge of the temple, an almost invariable adjunct of the village or a central place round which the inhabitants gathered together for communal life. Grants of land were made to the "Assembly" by the king or by other benefactors and if the members of that body failed in their duty, a fine was imposed upon every member by certain officers specially appointed by the king. The "Assembly's" powers were indeed very large. It had under it a body of arbitrators who wrote the tank accounts and collected maintenance charges in respect of tanks. These accounts had to be submitted to the "Assembly" and had to be proved to be correct and honest records.

Another inscription registers the construction of a mandapa in which were located a school, a hostel for the students and a hospital. The students were provided with food, bathing oil on saturdays and oil for lamps. The hospital was provided with 15 beds and had an establishment of a physician, a surgeon, two servants to fetch drugs and do other services for the hospital, two servants for nursing the patients and a general servant for the school, hostel and hospital. There is also an account of the medicines to be kept always in stock.

107. The Pandyas :—The Pandyan kingdom comprised the Madura and the Tinnevelly districts. The capital city Madura was held by Mahamadan governors from about 1311 to 1358 A. D.

108. The Cheras :—The Chera or Kerala kingdom comprised the Malabar region. Tradition faintly records that a number emigrated from Malabar to Egypt and settled on the banks of the Nile. It may, however, be safely inferred from this that Southern India had at least regular commercial intercourse with the Nile country.

109. Vijayanagar :— During the 14th century, the new Hindu state of Vijayanagar arose and dominated the whole of South India until its fall in 1565.

110. The Pallavas :—Between the 4th and the 8th centuries, the ancient southern states were overshadowed by a vigourous dynasty of unknown origin, the Pallavas.

They had their capital at Kanchi. They attained their maximum power in the 7th century when they destroyed the Chalukyas. The rock-cut caves in the Trichinopoly rock are attributed to them.

The stone inscription of Rajasimha II discovered in a Pallava temple on the hill at Panamalai in the South Arcot district mentions that the sage Asvatthaman Droni (The Drona of the Mahabharata also had a son called Asvatthaman Droni) had a son Vallava (Pallava)—the V and the P have almost the same form in the Grantha script, the script of the inscription—from whom came into existence the great Pallava family whose members are stated to have washed away their sins by performing the Asvamedha sacrifices, and who belonged to the Bharadvaja Vamsa. A famous king among them was Rajasimha who was a great devotee of Siva and under whose care the tree of Dharma thrived even though it was oppressed by the hot sun, viz., the Kali age.

111. It will not be out of place to state here that the early history of the Deccan, very little of which has yet been brought to light, has been peculiarly uniform in the growth and decay of small kingdoms. The comparatively peaceful and longlived years of the kingdoms may be said to have favoured the development of South Indian art and literature and the erection of the numerous temples abounding in the land. The south Indian states have practically been exclusive of northern India. Very little is known about South Indian history as such; hence the meagre information given in this volume.*

The ancient state of Travancore continues to remain to this day almost what it was in the past.

---

* The reader's attention is invited to the author's forthcoming book "The History of Trichinopoly prior to the British Occupation" where a fuller account of the ancient South Indian states is given.

CHAPTER XIX

The Mussalman Conquests.

112. Arabia in the 6th century A. D. :—In the 6th century A. D., Arabia was chiefly inhabited by tribes of nomads who depended for their living on their flocks and herds and whose principal occupation seems to have been warfare and plunder. Very little is known about their religion, except perhaps that they all held in reverence the Kaaba, the temple of the black image, in Mecca. The hereditary custodians of this temple were the Koraish, of one of whom was born Mahomed the Prophet, in A. D. 570.

113. Mahomed :—As a little boy, Mahomed seems to have possessed a reflective mind. He probably felt, like Bhagavan Buddha, the shams of every-day life, and a thirst for reform seems to have taken possession of his serious mind. In his 25th year he entered the service of a rich lady, who, fascinated with the handsome bearing and noble features of the youth, soon married him. As his contemplative tendencies increased, he retired to a cave to indulge the more in meditation and prayer.

114. The religion of Islam :— Dissatisfied with the idolatry of his countrymen, equally dissatisfied with the bloody rituals of Judaism and having seen the baser forms of Christianity as manifested by the multitude who were just beginning to flock round the banner of Jesus, Mahomed resolved to attempt a reform by which religion would be purged of all its gross elements. Finally he declared that he had a mission on earth to perform. He proclaimed with no uncertain voice " There is only Allah the Lord, and I Mahomed am His prophet. "

115. The Hijra :—As he began to preach his new gospel, he was persecuted and was finally obliged in 622 A. D. to save his life by escaping from Mecca. The year of his escape begins the Mussalman era and is called the Hijra.

116. Propaganda :—Mahomed, who had till now been advocating persuasion as the only legitimate means of spreading his faith, began to employ force to propagate the new religion. In 6 years, he had a following of 1,500 soldiers. Before his death in 632 A. D. all Arabia was under his control. The idea of world-conquest soon took possession of the Mahamadan mind. Egypt and all northern Africa were soon overrun and within a century after the death of Mahomed Spain and even France had been penetrated into.

117. The Occupation of Sindh :—Nor were the new religionists slow to turn their arms towards India the land of temptations. By 664 Persia was occupied and a Mahamadan army advanced as far as Kabul. In 712 A. D. Mahamad Bin Kasim of Basra conquered Sindh and invaded Rajputana. Bappa, lord of Mewar, nephew of the Pramara Rajput chief of Malwa, a boy of just 15 summers, with his warrior nature and heaven-bestowed weapons, seemed as leader sent by Durga Herself to guard Her land from foreigners. He drove the enemy before him, captured Ghazni and became the hero of the army. This was but the beginning of the long struggle in which the Rajputs fought the Muslim arms, a srtuggle in which heroic deeds were wrought alike by Hindu and Mussalman, a struggle to which both may look back with pride, as part of the making of modern India.

118. The spread of Islam:—It cannot, however, be explained how a new religion spread so rapidly with so much enthusiasm among the Arabs; nor how it aroused so quickly the zeal of a warlike people and made them invincible. The spread of a new religion is one of the mysteries of human nature which do not readily yield their secrets to attempts at summary explanation.

CHAPTER XX.

The Punjab occupation.

119. The first Indian province with the exception of Sindh permanently occupied by the Mussalmans was the Punjab annexed by Sultan Mahamad of Ghazni in about A. D. 1021. From the closing years of the 12th century, when the conquest of Hindustan was systematically undertaken, a stream of Muslim strangers began to flow into the plains of India till about the 18th century, profoundly changing the character of the population over immense areas.

120. The sultans of Ghazni:—In the early part of the 10th century, a Turkish slave of a chief of Korassan, whose work was said to have been to amuse his master by tumbling and tricks of legardemain, incurred the serious displeasure of his master and escaped to Ghazni where he established himself as the unquestioned ruler of a small principality. The third ruler of Ghazni was Amir Sabaktajin who came to power in A. D. 977.

121. Sabaktagin :—Amir Sabaktagin, as soon as he felt himself secure in his home beyond the mountains, began to make raids into the territory of the Rajput Jayapal. The latter retaliated by invading Ghazni. But, in the cold season, owing to an unusual downpour ot rain and a heavy thunderstorm, Jayapal lost many of his men and purchased an ignominious peace. In despair he promised to give the Amir 50 elephants and a large sum of money. When he came back to his own country, he refused the payment of the blackmail and formed a confederacy of the Rajput chiefs. , Sabaktagin descended from the hills and in a pitched battle defeated Jayapal and his comrades.

122. Sultan Mahamad of Ghazni:-In A. D. 997 Sabaktagin died and was succee ded by his son Sultan Mahamad of Ghazni. Urged by religious zeal and love of plunder. he seems to have conceived the mad project of islamising all India and of carrying on a holy war against that country To this end, he invaded India nearly 17 times.

123. Peshawar (A. D 1001) :—Jayapal was the old foe of his father against whom Mahamad first declared war. Jayapal was defeated at the battle of Peshawar, and being too proud to outlive his fame, placed his son Anangapal on the gaddi and went by fire to Swarga.

124. Multan (A. D. 1005) :—Anangapal was defeated by Mahamad at Peshawar in 1005 and Multan passed into Muslim hands.

125. Bhimnagar :—In A. D. 1008, Anangapal, though aided by the Rajput chiefs of Gwalior, Ujjain, Kalanjar, Kanouj, Delhi and Ajmere, was again defeated at Peshawar by Mahamad after a battle of 40 days. This decisive victory was followed up by the plunder of the famous temple of Bhimnagar or Nagarkot. "Among the booty was a house of white silver, like to the houses of rich men, the length of which was thirty yards and the breadth fifteen. It could be taken to pieces and put together again."

126. Kanouj:—In A. D. 1018 Mahamad again invaded India and suddenly arrived at the city of Baran (Bulandshahr). The Raja submitted and accepted the religion of Islam. "The sultan gave orders that all the temples should be burned with naphtha and fire and levelled with the ground."

Mahamad then marched on and in 1019 A. D. appeared unexpectedly at the gates of the magnificent and wealthy city of Kanouj. Raja Rajyapal submitted, but all the temples in the city were destroyed. Mahamad next captured Mathura and returned to Ghazni.

127. The Chandel submission:— Many Hindu princes, incensed at the un-Hindu submission of Rajyapal, marched against him and killed him. He was succeeded by his son Trilochanpal. Mahamad heard of this and in the autumn of 1019 turned back to India and met in open battle Ganda Chandel who had assembled a huge army. Each side was afraid of the other and long delayed the opening of hostilities. But at night the Raja got afraid and fled away leaving his camp and 580 elephants to the sultan.

In A. D. 1021, Mahamad again entered the Chandel territory and wrested from Ganda the fort of Kalanjar. In the same year he defeated Jayapal II, son of Anangapal, at Lahore and wrested from him that city.

128. Somnath :—In A. D. 1023, Mahamad invested the shrine of Somnath in Saurashtra. In the dreadful slaughter, the sacred lingam, about 5 yards high, one of the most holy ones in India, was smashed, and parts of it were taken to Ghazni and cast down at the threshold of the great mosque to be trodden underfoot.

129. Multan :—In A. D. 1027, Mahamad attacked the Jats at Multan and defeated them.

130. Mahamad's greatness :—During the rest of his life Mahamad was occupied with troubles at home. He died in A. D. 1030. He was the most distinguished warrior of his time. His success in arms in almost every battle that he fought and the good order that prevailed in his kingdom in spite of his numerous absences from it mark him out as a great statesman. He founded the university of Ghazni and liberally patronised learned men. He is also famous for the magnificence of his court and buildings.

131. The Ghor dynasty :—The cruelties practised by Bahram, one of Mahamad's successors, on a chieftain of Ghor, an obscure principality in the Hindu Kush, were terribly avenged in A. D. 1150 when Ghazni was sacked for seven days and nights and all its splendid buildings destroyed. The next Ghor chief was

Sultan Ghias-ud-din, whose younger brother, Mahamad, having reduced Ghazni to obedience, turned his attention to the rich plains of India.

132. Lahore passes into Ghor hands :—This disaster did not immediately deprive the dynasty of Ghazni of the Indian province of Lahore. Khusru Malik, the last prince of the house of Sabaktagin, retained Lahore till A. D. 1187, when he was expelled by Sultan Mahamad Ghor. It should be remembered that Lahore was the sole Mussalman province in India acquired by Mahamad Ghazni, while he made no attempt to hold the regions in the interior which he overran in the course of his raids.

CHAPTER XXI.

The effect on India of the Mussalman incursions.

133. In spite of the seventeen invasions of Sultan Mahamad of Ghazni, India remained essentially Hindu, and the interior Hindu kingdoms did survive the passing storms and were unmolested in conducting their affairs in their own fashion. Except in Sindh in the 8th century and in the Punjab in the 11th century, no considerable body of foreigners settled in India, and not till after 1200 A. D. did any Mussalman seriously think of establishing a permanent Indian dominion.

It should, however, be said that the Hindus had worked out for themselves a very high degree of civilisation during centuries of isolation (other than commercial) from the world outside. The advent of the Mussalmans, more warlike but less civilised than the Hindus, brought the latter suddenly into contact with a new state of things and the loss of national liberty brought about intellectual stagnation and the consequent corruption which are discernible even to this day.

134. Surviving Hindu kingdoms:- At this time, the great powers of northern India were not the same as in the past. The new groups of Rajputs and other powers may be named as.

i. Rahtores of Kanouj:—The last Rahtore was Raja Jayachandra.

ii. Tomaras or Tuars of Delhi:— Anangapal, a Tomara chief, probably a relation of the old Anangapal referred to in the previous chapter, beautified the ancient city of Delhi, the Indraprastha of the Mahabharata, with handsome buildings. He erected a group of 27 fine temples, from the materials of which, the Kutb-Minar was later on built.

A grandson of this Anangapal by his mother was Raja Jayachandra of

Kanouj. Grandson also of Anangapal by his mother was Prithvi, the son of a Chohan chief of Ajmere. Prithvi succeeded Anangapal, according to the latter's wish, in A. D. 1164. Jayachandra put forth his equal claim and bitter feud arose between the two proud princes. Round them grouped themselves the hot-blooded Rajput chiefs in rival hosts, even as the rulers of India did when Duryodhana and Yudhishthira struggled for the throne of Indraprastha in pre-historic times. But around Jayachandra not only Rajaputras were gathered. The semitic faces of the Pathans and the Turks mingled with the Aryan faces of the Rajputs, and in the fratricidal strife, the Mussalman, eager to make firm his footing, takes a willing part. Sultan Mahamad Ghor is watching from Lahore, his eye upon the throne of the Pandavas. Raja Prithvi was triumphant in the fight.

iii. Chouhans of Ajmere;

iv. Palas and Senas of Bengal;

v. Chalukya Baghilas of Saurashtra;

vi. Sumeras of Sindh.

135. Want of political unity among the Hindu kingdoms:—The above states were independent of one another. When they had not a war with the Muslim on hand, they kept their swords sharp against one another. Whenever they formed a confederacy in a desperate emergency, it was loosely held together and easily dissolved.

CHAPTER XXII.

Sultan Mahamad Ghor in India.

136. Before Sultan Mahamad Ghor obtained possession of Lahore in 1187, as stated in § 132 supra, he had attacked and captured Multan in 1175. Elated by this success he marched into Guzerat in 1178, but was signally defeated by the Baghilas.

137. Raja Prithvi vs. Mahamad Ghor :—But the flame of his ambition only burnt the hotter, and he possessed the eager desire of enjoying the plunder and acquiring the sovereignty of the rich Rajput kingdoms. Onward pressed the Afghan and captured Bhatinda. The Lion of Delhi, Raja Prithvi, awoke as if from sleep and suddenly sprang to meet the foe. The enemy was rolled back, broken, on Lahore (A. D. 1191).

138. Raja Prithvi vs. Mahamad Ghor for a second time :—Two years had passed ; again Mahamad threatened. Many a Rajput chief came galloping to meet the call of Prithvi, the fiery-hearted children of the king, but alas! Jayachandra, Prithvi's cousin, came not. On the banks of the river Ghuggur, the same hallowed spot whence the aggressor was driven back so forcibly two years ago, Prithvi and his men assembled to meet the serried ranks of the Muslims. "Twice the sun set on that scene of slaughter, and the crimson western rays were thrown back yet more crimsoned from the ranks of the dead that lay in long rows on the blood-besprinkled earth. The sun rose again on the third morning and saw yet once more the strife commence ; at eve of that third day the fight was over. Thirteen thousands of the warriors of Mewar and thousands more of Delhi's noblest and bravest lay asleep on the banks of the Ghuggur. But Raja Prithvi, charging with desperate courage, time after time, on the very crest of the wave of steel, was carried by his impetuosity far into the ranks of the enemy, and, seeking death in vain, was dragged from his steed by countless hands, ere he could free himself from his fallen war-horse, and held helpless by his triumphant foes. Sharp taunt from Mahamad's lips was met by proud dauntless answer. High was reared the noble head for the last time; the laughing lips sent out a shaft of jesting scorn. Out flashed a dagger, quickly plunged into the captive's breast; one moment more he stood, while all men held their breath, and then fell headlong and lay prone in death, as falls a forest tree before the woodsman's axe."

139. Further conquest of northern India:—With Prithvi perished the throne of the Pandavas, and in the place of the Lotus flower now waved the Crescent. And the rest of the story takes not long to tell. The pathans swept onwards and took Delhi by assault. Kanouj was added to the Muslim empire in, 1195. Benares soon fell and 1197 saw the proud Baghilas of Guzerat, who nineteen years previously baffled the Muslim, fall. In

1203 Kalanjar, the strong fortress of the Chandels, capitulated.

140. Mahamad Ghor's death:— Sultan Mahamad Ghor returned to Ghazni late in 1203; he came back to India in 1205 to suppress a revolt in the Punjab. On his way back, he was murdered on the road, a fitting end to the murderer of Raja Prithvi.

CHAPTER XXIII.

The Sultanate of Delhi.

141. Sultan Mahamad Ghor was largely indebted to his general Kutb-ud-din, a Turk, whom the Sultan had formerly purchased as a slave. It was he who captured Benares. When Mahamad returned to Ghazni in 1203, Kutb-ud-din was left in charge of the operations in India. The capture of Kalanjar was his work. He was at Delhi when Mahamad was assassinated; his successor Sultan Ghiyas-ud-din Mahamad Ghor of Ghor and Ghazni not only released Kutb-ud-din from slavery, but also conferred on him the title of Sultan.

142. Sultan Kutb-ud-din of Delhi:- Sultan Kutb-ud-din may be regarded from 1206 as an independent Indian sovereign, the first of a long line of sultans who sat on the throne of the Pandavas at Delhi.

CHAPTER XXIV

Conclusion.

143. Having thus far studied in detail the history of ancient India, it will be quite in the fitness of things to briefly review the outstanding political and social features in the ancient history of the land.

144. The period of pre-Mussalman activities in the land may be divided into (1) the Vedic ages, (2) the post-Vedic or the pre-Buddhistic ages, (3) the Buddhistic ages, (4) the post-Buddhistic ages and (5) the period of Mussalman aggression.

145. In the Vedic ages, which form a time when the very beginnings of history fail to be traced, the Aryans in India had attained a very high degree of civilisation and their society was an established organisation.

The country was divided into about fiftysix kingdoms every one of which had its own king. These kingdoms were not only independent of one another but also of the central Government. There are very few instances when the Chakravarti ever interfered with the internal administration of these independent kingdoms except perhaps on occasions of Asvamedha and other sacrifices when special tributes were levied. The nearest parallel that can be conceived of is found in the present-day administration of the U. S. A. The various States composing the U. S. A. are practically independent of one another, even in the matter of passing their own laws and regulations. These States do not even recognise a national holiday, not even Christmas day or the Independence day. The ancient Hindu kings were advised by competent ministers well-learned in the art of political Government. Popular grievances were personally heard by the several kings and immediately redressed and no criminal was ever left unpunished. In fact the king recognised it as his duty to prevent crime and, if he failed in this, to at least bring the offenders to book. If he failed in this the most sacred of all duties, the sins of the criminals devolved on him and he became unfit to maintain the trust reposed in him, viz., the protection of the people.

Hindu society was fundamentally divided into the four castes and one caste was not to take upon itself under any circumstances the duties of another, whatever may be the keenness of the struggle for existence. The mandate in the Bhagavad Gita re-stated with greater emphasis by Manu and the author of Sakuntala seem to have been scrupulously observed, and the consequent non-conflict of interests in the absence of competition was the cause of the Aryan's peaceful pursuits.

Even in warfare, the ancient Hindu conception of what is called धर्मयुद्ध was based upon a high standard of morality. The test of strength was not large numbers, nor was it the possession of steel and fire, but manliness based upon physica and mental qualities and the power to use Divine weapons with the knowledge of mantras. Humbled enemies were always treated with the honour due to their rank, non-combatants and women were always respected and agricultural operations never hampered by military marches.

Their religion was the Sanatana Dharma, the most universal of all religions, with perfect toleration for the beliefs of all. "From the high spiritual flights of the Vedanta philosophy, of which the latest discoveries of science seem like echoes, to the low ideas of idolatry with its multifarious mythology, the agnosticism of the Buddhists and the atheism of the Jains, each and all have a place in the Hindu's religion." It has no location in place or time; it is infinite like the God it preaches; its sun shines upon the followers of Krishna and of Christ; on saints and sinners alike; it is not Brahmanic or Buddhistic, Christian or Mahamadan, but the sum-total of all these and still has infinite space for development; in its catholicity it embraces every human being, in its infinite arms, and finds a place for all from the lowest grovelling savage not far removed from the brute to the highest man towering by the virtues of his head and heart almost above humanity making society stand in awe of him and doubt his human nature. It is a religion which has no place for persecution or intolerance in its polity, which recognises divinity in every man and woman, and whose whole scope, whose whole force, is centred in aiding humanity to realise its own true divine nature. Religion has never been the crying need of India, and the Christians of foreign countries who are so fond of sending missionaries to save the soul of the heathen—why do they not try to save their bodies from destruction? They erect churches all through India, but the crying need in India is not, never was, religion,—the Indians have religion enough—it is bread that the suffering millions of India cry out today for, with parched throats.

Barring the fanatical attempts of a few Mussalman conquerors, there was never any organised attempt in pre-Mussalman India at proseletisation. The process of the Aryanisation of the non-Aryan elements in the land was slowly but surely going on for hundreds and thousands of years till the deprivation of national independence by the less civilised but more warlike Mussalmans brought about a sudden stagnation. It is the Mussalman who was the first non-Aryan to enter India, who refused to come under Aryan influence and who to this day preserves a distinct and separate national existence of his own.

Nor was social service to the poor and the needy and the miserable ever neglected. The basis of charity was शरणागतरक्षणम् and the later teaching of Jesus "Ask and it shall be given, knock and it shall be opened" seems to have taken a very strong hold of the popular mind in the Vedic ages.

Last of all, Aryan India produced in the Vedic ages a set of intellectual giants whose works on all kinds of sciences are indeed marvellous; their works on philosophy stand second to those of no other heroes of any other country, ancient or modern.

146. In the post-Vedic ages, when the type of political sovereignty was gradually decaying through the ignorance of adharmika kings, the forest Rishis disappeared and a cleavage arose between the Gnanakandin and the Karmakandin. The assimilation of the non-Aryan elements was creating new sections in Hindu society to which Vedic orthodoxy failed to make religious ministrations, because of the wiping off of the forest Rishis and the consequent loosening of Vedic orthodoxy from its Upanishadic basis. A social revolution was almost imminent and the situation was saved by the advent of the Mahapurushas Mahavira and Gautama.

147. While these religious reformers

were essentially Hindus by birth, by study and by training, they perceived the powerlessness of Vedic ordhodoxy and began to popularise religion. The mighty attempts to spread the gospel of love and toleration of the world-honoured Tathagata made by Asokavardhana, Kanishka and other Buddhist kings brought about wonderful results. But the contact with the numerous non-Aryan foreign invaders of the time brought into Hindu society outlandish manners and customs seeking to be infused into the views of the old life of India, and corrupting Hindu society to a great extent. And the very causes which helped to spread the gospel of Buddha brought about the downfall of Buddhism. Vedic ordhodoxy, under the aegis of the great Hindu kings, Samudra Gupta, Chandra Gupta Vikramaditya and Harshavardhana, began to reform and adapt itself to the changing needs of the times; and under the spiritual guidance of Bhagavan Sankaracharya and the political domination of the Rajaputras, the descendants of the ancient Kshatriyas, Vedic ordhodoxy was more firmly established in the land than ever.

148. At this stage of the history of ancient India rushed into the field the warlike Mussalman against the mild Hindu, and, as if by magic, deprived the latter almost suddenly of the political sovereignty of the land; and, as an inevitable result, **the process of Aryanisation came to an abrupt end.**

149. During centuries of isolation, other than commercial,—for India carried on even in those distant ages large trade with the foreign countries of China, Egypt and the Roman empire, the enormous profits of which attracted the hardy nations of western Europe to this ancient land,—the Hindus had developed for themselves a very high degree of civilisation the adamantine basis of which it has not yet been possible for the non-Aryan conquerors of the land even to shake; and the loss-of national independence brought about intellectual stagnation and the consequent corruption which are perceptible even to this day.

CHAPTER XXV

The sources of Indian History.

150. Before concluding this sketch of ancient Indian history, it will be well to say a few words on the sources of Indian history. In all countries the materials for the exact history of remote ages are scanty. Still more so is this the case regarding ancient India, because the people of ancient India, Aryans and non-Aryans alike, did not care to preserve records of their doings and hand them down to posterity. Metaphysical speculation was to them an absorbing passion. They would rather revel in literature and philosophy than in writing history. And the greatest among them were the Mantra-Drashtas, seers of Truth, sages or Rishis.

151. Although no formal histories as such were written, it must be noted that every Raja took pains to keep a record of his genealogy and a chronicle of his doings.

But most of these records must have disappeared owing to the numerous foreign invasions and the consequent wars. A few, however, seem to have been spared, such as Samudra Gupta's pillar at Allahabad, the Chola temple at Tanjore, the Mahavamsa chronicles of Ceylon, etc

152. Something about the doings of the people of ancient India and the condition of their society is also learnt from their literature, both religious and secular.

153. The Government Archaeological Department has at great pains been bringing to light plenty of information about the past from its excavation finds. Among these finds may be mentioned coins, inscriptions on stone and copper plates and monuments. The inscriptions on stone and copper plates are certainly real history written at a time when paper and binding were probably unknown.

154. It should not be forgotten that there are a few real histories of the past still extant, from which much useful information is derived. Chief among these are the Itihasas (the Ramayana and the Mahabharata of pre-historic times), the Harshacharita of Bana and the Rajatarangini of Kalhana.

155. The student of history is also indebted to foreign records for much of his information regarding the people of ancient India. He owes not a little to the Grecian and Chinese travellers and pilgrims who have been kind enough to leave behind them their impressions of the country.

156. Tradition is another fruitful source of our knowledge of the past of the country and according to some authorities the most truthful source.

157. Lastly, Mahamadan literary men, unlike the Hindus, had a strong passion for the writing of histories; though their records reveal traces of the very strong prejudice they had against the Hindus, they are yet very valuable, because they supply much of the information about the past of India that is so much needed.*

---

*The teacher should make use of some of these sources to illustrate his statements and to make his pupils realise that the history given to them is based on certain records which are accessible and which they can later on study more thoroughly.

Miss M. O. Davis, History Mistress, Edgbaston High School, sounds, however, a note of warning regarding the use of original sources in the teaching of history. She says that the true aim of a scholar should be the ability to find information rather than a good memory. "Useless details about archaeology must not be dragged in; local history, unless interesting, is better avoided and old historical remains must not be made into a fetish.

It is ridiculous to expect a child to reconstruct a vanished civilisation from such things as a man of science constructs a mammoth from one bone. For this would merely encourage the superstition that everything old must be valuable and interesting; in some teachers it may even lead to pedagogic absurdities. There is a recorded case of an ardent young lady teacher of English literature who, in dire necessity of something concrete to show her class, bottled some smoke and waved it enthusiastically before her pupils whilst she expounded Shelley's 'Cloud'. Quite as foolish thing are often done by the 'realistic' history teacher."

The teacher of history should therefore remember that first-hand material, when used only as illustrative matter, provides a vivid representation that somebody else's second-hand account can never give. A letter of Chatham's, for instance, must get a firmer grip than a precis of it by, say, Tout. "The historian trained on sources will come nearer to the kind of historian-politician Lord Morley seemed to have in his mind when speaking recently at Manchester."

APPEN

- Vivaswan (Sun)
  - Vaivaswata Manu
    - Ikshwaku
      - Vikukshi
        - Trisanku (28 from Vivaswan)
          - Harischandra
            - Sagara (38 from Vivaswan)
              - Bhagiratha (42 from Vivaswan)
                - Rituparna (47 from Vivaswan)
                  - Balika (52 from Vivaswan)
                    - Raghu (58 from Vivaswan)
                      - Aja
                        - Dasaratha
                          - Bharata
                            - Taksha
                          - Rama married Sita
                            - Kusa
                              - Maru (20 from Kusa)
                                - Kritanjaya (49 from Kusa)
                                  - Sumitra (57 from Kusa) about 56 B. C.
                            - Lava
      - Nimi
        - Janaka
          - Siradhwaja or Janaka
            - Sita

- Rajput Chiefs of Jaipur, Marwar, Bikanir, Nerwar (Nala), Amber, Bundi, Kotah, Kanouj, Dhara, Mhow, Ujjain, Suru, Kalian, Multan and Malwa.
- Agnikula Pramara (Mewar)
  - Chandragupta Maurya
    - Asokavardhana
      - Brihadratha
- Agnikula Purihara (Mundore)
- Agnikula Solanki (Anhulwarra)
- Agni Chau (Ajm
  - P

Delhi pass

D I X I.

Soma (Moon) married Tara

Budha married Ila

Pururavas married Urvasi

Vijaya — Jahnu — Gadhi — Visvamitra — Jamadagni — Parasurama

Ayus — Nahusha — Yayati

Yadu

Puru

Kroshtu

Madhu (26 from Yadu)

Vrishni (39 from Yadu)

Viduratha — Akrura

Vasudeva (7 from Vrishni)

Sri Krishna

Dushyanta married Sakuntala

Bharata

Bharadwaja

Rantideva — Hastin

Kuru

Devapi — Jarasandha — Santanu

Bhishma

Dhritarashtra — Vidura — Pandu

Yudhishtira

Parikshit

Rajapala (2915 years from Parikshit) slain by Sukmanta

la
an
e)

Vikramaditya Tuar who slew Sukmanta

Anangapal Tuar (A. D. 792)

Anangapal Taur (A. D. 1164)

; I T H V I

into Moslem hands—A. D. 1193.

APPENDIX II.

LINE OF TIME.

Date	Period	Phase	Event
B.C. 2000			Aryans and Non-Aryans.
			Aryan contact with Dravidian.
			Post-Vedic Ages.
700			Mahavira.
624			Buddha.
600	EMPIRE OF MAGADHA	Rise of Buddhism.	Magadha Kingdom.
500	EMPIRE OF MAGADHA	Rise of Buddhism.	Persian Exploration of the Indus Valley.
326	EMPIRE OF MAGADHA	Rise of Buddhism.	Alexander's Invasion.
305	EMPIRE OF MAGADHA	Rise of Buddhism.	Selucus's Invasion.
272	EMPIRE OF MAGADHA	Rise of Buddhism.	Asokavardhana.
256	EMPIRE OF MAGADHA	Rise of Buddhism.	First Buddhist Council.
184	EMPIRE OF MAGADHA	Decline of Buddhism and Formation of New Hinduism.	Pushyamitra Sunga.
155	EMPIRE OF MAGADHA	Decline of Buddhism and Formation of New Hinduism.	Menander's Invasion.
	EMPIRE OF MAGADHA	Decline of Buddhism and Formation of New Hinduism.	Saka Invasion.
72	EMPIRE OF MAGADHA	Decline of Buddhism and Formation of New Hinduism.	Kanwa Dynasty.
	EMPIRE OF MAGADHA	Decline of Buddhism and Formation of New Hinduism.	Yueh-Chi Invasion.
	EMPIRE OF MAGADHA	Decline of Buddhism and Formation of New Hinduism.	Andhra Kingdom.
A.D. 120	EMPIRE OF MAGADHA	Decline of Buddhism and Formation of New Hinduism.	Kanishka.
320	HINDU KINGDOMS	Decline of Buddhism and Formation of New Hinduism.	Gupta Dynasty.
399	HINDU KINGDOMS	Decline of Buddhism and Formation of New Hinduism.	Fa Hian.
430	HINDU KINGDOMS	Decline of Buddhism and Formation of New Hinduism.	White Hun Invasion.
528	HINDU KINGDOMS	Decline of Buddhism and Formation of New Hinduism.	Yasodharman.
606	HINDU KINGDOMS	Decline of Buddhism and Formation of New Hinduism.	Harshavardhana.
608	HINDU KINGDOMS	Decline of Buddhism and Formation of New Hinduism.	Pulikesin II (Chalukya).
621	HINDU KINGDOMS	Decline of Buddhism and Formation of New Hinduism.	Yuan Chung.
712	HINDU KINGDOMS	Decline of Buddhism and Formation of New Hinduism.	Mussalman Occupation of Sindh.
	HINDU KINGDOMS	Decline of Buddhism and Formation of New Hinduism.	Rajput Ascendancy.
788	HINDU KINGDOMS	Decline of Buddhism and Formation of New Hinduism.	Sankaracharya.
986	HINDU KINGDOMS		Mahamadan Incursions into the Punjab.
988	HINDU KINGDOMS		Rajput Attack on Ghazni.
997	HINDU KINGDOMS		Sultan Mahamad of Ghazni.
1001–1027	HINDU KINGDOMS		Sultan Mahamad of Ghazni's Indian Expeditions.
1150	HINDU KINGDOMS		Ghazni passes into Ghor hands.
1187	HINDU KINGDOMS		Indian Provinces of Ghazni pass into Ghor hands.
1191	MUSLIM RULE		Sultan Mahamad Ghor defeated by Raja Prithvi.
1193	MUSLIM RULE		Sultan Mahamad Ghor defeats Raja Prithvi and the Throne of the Pandavas passes into Muslim hands.
1197	MUSLIM RULE		Guzerat falls before the Muslims.
1203	MUSLIM RULE		Kalanjar falls before the Muslims.
1206	MUSLIM RULE		Sultan Mahamad Ghor of Ghor and Ghazni dies and Sultanate of Delhi founded.

APPENDIX III.

"They are very wise men—the Orientalists; they are psychometrical adepts. Place anything before them, a rag, a thighbone, a tooth, a coin or a piece of stone and they will spin you an interminable yarn of the man, of the beast or of the people—their history, physical, mental, moral, political, literary, economic, industrial, religious, as if they were the very Makers of the objects they operate upon. They would search for history in a book of sacrificial hymns like the Rig Veda, in ritualistic manuals like the Yajur Veda, in a book of psalmody like the Sama Veda, in a book of rhymes and charms like the Atharva Veda. They would seek for "historic finds" in moral text-books like the Smritis, in sacred epics like the Ramayana and the Mahabharata; nay, they profess to give you the life and thoughts of a nation from its grammar like the Mahabhashya, from its philosophical works like the Vedanta literature, from its medical books like Vagbhata, Susruta and Charaka; and wonderful to relate, they find history in treatises upon logic like Tarkasangraha, in mathematical works like the Leelavati and the Bijaganita ! ! Nothing is too trivial, too humble, too insignificant for them ; their historical appetite is omnivorous.

"I would give anything to know what they might feel like if an orthodox Brahman or a Charvaka Atheist were to place before the English Christian reading world an English version of the Hebrew Bible ; if he should have the additional advantage of only a nodding acquaintance with the language ; if he should never have set his eye on the people whose revealed scriptures he professes to further reveal ; if he should never have come across the real sacred books of the East ; if he should have come into contact only with the lowest strata of the nation or with unprincipled renegades to the faith of their fathers ; if he should not even dream of access to the higher classes, their homes, their life, their words, their acts, their joys, their sorrows, their virtues, their vices, their faith and their scepticism ; if he should be imbued with a supremely high notion of his omniscience, of his unerring keenness, of his literary infallibility ; if he should take it for granted that his race is the chosen one, that his religion is the only true one and that the others are false, that his people are destined to march for ever in the fore-front of civilisation, prosperity and power. Now what would the orthodox English Christians or the devout Bishops and Archbishops think of such a version of the Holy Bible, embellished to boot with original commentaries, remarks, reconciliations, judgments, *ex cathedra*, based mostly on the unhealthy fumes of his imagination and prejudices? How would the English nation like to have its history written, say 5,000 years hence, from stray coins, from mouldering skeletons, from moss-covered pieces of stone and architecture, from its "Book of Common Prayer", from its "Book of Psalmody", from the "Paradise Lost" of Milton, from the "Holy Living" of Taylor, from Abbot's Shakespearian Grammar, from Jevon's Logic, from Masson's British Philosophy, from Barnard Smith's Arithmetic, from Todhunter's Algebra and Geometry, from Webster's Dictionary, from its scientific, medical, industrial and mechanical treatises, and other decaying rubbish of a forgotten nation buried under the mounds of the past?

"That is exactly how the true Aryan feels when he reads translations like those of Max Muller, Griffith and others or original critical estimates like those of the Orientalists. Western historians depict in glowing colours and sneering language how Mahamad of Ghazni destroyed the idol of Somnath ; but Weber and others essay to shatter to pieces the faith of millions, their guide here and their hope hereafter. Well, as he soweth, so shall he reap. My opinion of the whole class and of their Indian parasites is the same as what I expressed in the preface to my "Life and Teachings of Sri Ramanuja", and I quote it for the benefit of those who have not come across that book.

"'What care I about your coins and inscriptions, your pillars and mounds, the dry bones of history ? To me it is of far more importance how a man lived and worked among his fellows than when and where he was born and died, where he was at a particular date, when he wrote such and such a book, whether he was tall or short, dark or fair, single or married, a flesh-eater or a vegetarian, a teetotaller or no, what particular dress he affected, and so on. And yet, more important still it is to me what a man thought and wrote, than how he lived and died.

"'Orientalists ! Heaven save me from the

brood. Mischief enough they have done, those human ghouls that haunt the charnel houses of Antiquity, where rot the bones of men and events of the dead past. They have played sad havoc with the fair traditions of our forefathers, that placed ideas before facts and theories and the development of a nation's heart before "historical finds" or "valuable discoveries". Many a young man of promise they have turned away to paths uncongenial * * * * * * You will find no such antiquarian twaddle in my book.'

"Well do they fit in with the lines of Tennyson :

'Those monstrous males that carve
the living hound,
And cram him with the fragments
of the grave,
Or in the dark dissolving human heart,
And holy secrets of this microcosm,
Dabbling a shameless hand with
shameful jest,
Encarnalise their spirits.'

"Gladly would I exchange shiploads of them for one Sir Edwin Arnold.

* * * *

"Alas! The history of India by the Rev. Dr. Sinclair is at present more authoritative in the eyes of the school-boys than the Ramayana of Valmeeki or the Puranas of Vyasa. The history of Sanskrit literature by Messrs. Max Muller, Weber, Monier Williams, MacDonnel, etc., is the last word upon the writings of the Aryans, religious and secular. Translations are quoted and the originals are decried or are unknown. Verily, we are in the iron age, in the ever-downward cycle of the Kaliyuga.

"I hold that any history of India worth reading ought to be written by a true-hearted Hindu; I hold that the sacred books of the Hindus ought to be translated by a Hindu, by a Brahman, by one that has faith in the virtues and manhood of his people, in the wisdom and philanthropy of his forefathers, by one that combines in himself a deep and comprehensive knowledge of the literature and traditions of his country, and of that to which he means to convey his message—but never by one of alien faith, nor a follower of Christianity without Christ, nor an Apostate seeking to curry favour with the ruling race and the leaders of western thought."—*C. R. Srinivasa Aiyangar B. A., in his "Introduction to the Study of the Ramayana."*